Dante's
Drama of the Mind

A MODERN READING OF
THE *PURGATORIO*

Dante's
Drama of the Mind

A MODERN READING OF
THE *PURGATORIO*

BY FRANCIS FERGUSSON

GREENWOOD PRESS, PUBLISHERS
WESTPORT, CONNECTICUT

Library of Congress Cataloging in Publication Data

Fergusson, Francis.
    Dante's drama of the mind.

    Reprint. Originally published: Princeton : Princeton
University Press, 1968.
    Includes bibliographical references.
    1. Dante Alighieri, 1265-1321. Purgatorio. I. Title.
PQ4447.F4 1981   851'.1   81-4190
ISBN 0-313-23034-X (lib. bdg.)   AACR2

First published in 1953. This is a reprint of the second
printing, 1968.

Reprinted by arrangement with Princeton University
Press.

Reprinted in 1981 by Greenwood Press
A division of Congressional Information Service, Inc.
88 Post Road West, Westport, Connecticut 06881

Printed in the United States of America

10 9 8 7 6 5 4 3 2 1

ॐ FOREWORD

THE READING of the *Divine Comedy*, like the reading of Shakespeare, has no end: one does not reach the point where it is possible to say that we see what is in it. That is not because Dante's poem is obscurely written, for the most innocent reader can begin to enjoy it at once. It is because of two properties of great poetry which it possesses to a unique degree: inner coherence, and the property of illuminating the reader's most intimate experience at every stage of life. One soon sees that beneath the ceaseless movement of the verse an order is unfolding; but the order continues to unfold in new ways. And its meaning for us appears in a slightly different light every time we look at it.

This book is the unforeseen result of my having read the *Divine Comedy* off and on for about twenty-five years. Between 1934 and 1947 I read it with small groups of students at Bennington College. A certain fairly stable view of the way the poem is composed, and of the way it is intended to be read, gradually emerged. My purpose is to explain this view of the developing form of the poem; in short, to facilitate the endless, always surprising, yet surer and surer process of exploration.

I have several reasons for focussing upon the *Purgatorio* rather than the *Inferno* or the *Paradiso*. The *Inferno* is better known and more immediately effective. I suppose that anyone with a little interest in Dante (anyone who might look at this book) will have some impression of it. Its magic is like the inspired, unplaced visions of modern art, easy for us. But by itself it gives a false impression of the *Comedy*. For Dante, no poetic vision was a sufficient end in itself, however powerful and beautiful; and the *Inferno* demands the other canticles. As for the *Paradiso*, it is much the most difficult of the three. One may start to enjoy it at once, but it is the last part of the *Comedy* which could be discussed with any confidence.

The *Purgatorio* is the transitional canticle, in many respects the center of the whole *Comedy*. It is the tragic and triumphant answer to Hell, and the preparation for the beatific vision. It is the drama of the discovery of the order of Dante's vision, and also the drama of the making of the poem. There Dante most unmistakably presents his own spirit at work; if we cannot glimpse it, it is not through any failure of art or candor on his part. Moreover, the *Purgatorio,* though "hoarse with long silence," as Dante said of Virgil, might have much to say to our time if it were better known. Mr. T. S. Eliot recommends Dante as the best model for contemporary poets. The *Purgatorio* has light to shed also upon history and its making; upon psychology, ethics, and education; upon politics and the transmission of our tradition. There are many reasons for learning to read it; it is a central clue.

I owe a great deal to several writers on Dante, and I have tried to indicate my debts to them in the course of the book and in the Notes at the back of the volume.

I wish to record my gratitude to the Committee for the Princeton Seminars in Literary Criticism, the late Donald A. Stauffer and Professors Richard Blackmur, Whitney J. Oates, and Ira O. Wade, for the valuable opportunity to present a six-weeks' seminar on the *Purgatorio* to their group in the autumn of 1949.

Mr. Benjamin F. Houston, of the Princeton University Press, has taken care of the innumerable details of publication, and I am most grateful to him for his skill and his kindness.

Several chapters in approximately their present form have appeared in the *Hudson Review, Kenyon Review*, and *Thought.* I have to thank the editors of those publications for permission to reprint here.

F. F.

❧ A NOTE ON THE TRANSLATIONS IN THE TEXT

THE Italian quotations from the *Divine Comedy* throughout this book are taken from the Temple Classics edition. The translations are my own. I have versified them because I believe that a prose translation, even a literal one, is misleading.

In making my translations I have tried to take as few liberties as possible with the literal meaning, even when Dante's imagery seemed difficult or strange in English. I have not tried for strict and consistent rhymes, but instead I have sought to suggest the effect of *terza rima* by means of assonance. There is something to be said for this scheme in principle. *Terza rima* is very difficult in English, and strict rhyme in our language is likely to seem more artificial and insistent than it does in Dante's Italian. My purpose, however, was not to replace the original, or even to make an equivalent in English, but to lead the reader to savor Dante's own verses, and perhaps to try some translations of his own. Translating is one way to increased understanding and enjoyment.

I owe a special debt of gratitude to Professor Charles S. Singleton of Harvard, who has read my translations. He is not to be held responsible for my results, but I have been helped in many ways by his superb knowledge of the original which he generously made available to me, and by his advice and encouragement.

᷒ CONTENTS

CONTENTS

PART FOUR. TIME REDEEMED
(The Morning of the Fourth Day: Cantos XXVIII-XXXIII)

· x ·

PART ONE

THE PATHOS OF EARTH
(THE FIRST DAY: CANTOS I-IX)

ঽ঵ CHAPTER 1. THE METAPHOR OF
THE JOURNEY

For the first line of the first canto of the *Divine Comedy* Dante wrote:

> Nel mezzo del cammin di nostra vita
>
> (In the middle of the journey of our life)

There everything starts: in the middle of human life considered as a journey. There Dante was so lost and terrified that the journey to the realms beyond the grave became necessary for his salvation. But there too he found the strength and vision he required.

Dante knew that "the journey of our life" was a metaphor. He knew that the journey beyond the grave was a vastly extended metaphor also, in its literal meaning a fiction. But it was the miraculously right metaphor for his purposes, for what he had to show were the swarming journeys of human life with a clarity, vital intensity, and hidden order which seem to be indeed that of death, the aspect of eternity.

Knowing the fictiveness of his poem, knowing its sources, its manifold techniques, and all the subtle stratagems of its make-believe, he certainly did not believe it literally. But he believed, beyond our capacity for belief, in the truth which his fiction was devised to show. He tells Can Grande that his purpose was "to remove those living in this life from the state of misery, and lead them to the state of felicity." He reveals the truth of the human condition: the state of misery in the beginning of the poem, the state of felicity, after so many changing scenes, at the end. He does not preach: the journey speaks for him. But the journey has a double movement, the literal narrative and the movement of understanding, which is always going from the make-believe of the visionary scene to the truth beneath it: to the human spirit, on its way, or milling in some deathly eddy.

The notion of human life as a journey, and the related notion that the guides of the race must journey beyond the grave and meet the spirits of the ancestors in order to grasp their earthly way and ours, seems to be as old as the myth-making instinct itself. Dante likens his mission to the legendary missions of Aeneas and Paul, both of whom had to acquire the second, the post-mortem vision. Behind the legends of Aeneas's and Paul's journeys to the other world lie the myths of prehistoric culture-heroes, which were associated with *rites de passage*, ceremonies of initiation marking the stages of human life from the cradle to the grave. The *Divine Comedy* may be regarded as an initiation, or series of initiations, into the wisdom of the tribe. But Dante's tribe had an old and complex civilization, and Dante is not merely primitive. He is, at the same time, at least as sophisticated in his own way as the hero of a modern *Bildungsroman*: Hans Castorp, say, doing his reading in his mountain sanitarium, or one of Henry James's American pilgrims, undergoing his initiation on the "stage of Europe."

In the countless uses which Dante makes of metaphors of journeying, he never loses the primitive power of the metaphor, yet at the same time he employs it for the subtlest metaphysical and epistemological distinctions. All the journey-metaphors are based on the analogy, which the human mind finds very natural, between physical movement and the non-spatial action of the soul. The direct force of this analogy is unmistakable (for example) in Ulysses' narrative of his last ocean-voyage, in *Inferno*, Canto xxvi. But Ulysses' journey is in a carefully-controlled relation of analogy to Dante's journey down into Hell. It is also analogous to his subsequent journey up the Mount of Purgatory; but the journey into Hell is not continuous with the journey of purgation. The Pilgrim's transition from the one to the other is left mysterious, and each has its own validity as a metaphor for one aspect of earthly life. I have already mentioned the distinction between any of the journeys beyond the grave and the journey of this life. There are also the journeys of the making of the canticles, which are likened to sea-voyages, though *different* sea-voyages, in the opening sequences of the *Purgatorio* and the *Paradiso*. The reader too is supposed to be making a journey, at his peril, under Dante's guidance (*Paradiso*, Canto II, line 1):

> O voi, che siete in piccioletta barca,
>   desiderosi d'ascoltar, seguiti
>   retro al mio legno che cantando varca,
> tornate a riveder li vostri liti:
>   non vi mettete in pelago; chè forse,
>   perdendo me, rimarreste smarriti.

> (O you, who are there in your little boat,
>   longing to listen, following my way
>   behind my timbers singing as they go,
> turn you back to find your own coasts again:
>   do not trust to the open sea; for perhaps,
>   once losing me, you would be left astray.)

As one gets used to reading the *Divine Comedy*, one learns to see that Dante is continually correcting and amplifying one metaphorical journey with another; and by that means creating a sense of ceaseless life and movement, and of perpetually deepening, yet more and more closely-defined meaning.

II

One can see in a general way why Dante should have had to descend to the bottom of Hell before the other journeys became possible. Once in the terror of the Dark Wood, he had to explore the full import of that experience before his spirit was free to take another direction. And the vision of Hell is the occasion, the necessary preliminary to the other visions. Hell is the death which must precede rebirth, a moment which recurs by analogy through the whole poem:

a moment in that tragic rhythm which governs the movement of the *Divine Comedy* in the whole and in its parts.

After the release from Hell, the incommensurable journey of purgation can get under way; but we know that it does not reach the final Goal which Dante envisaged. The *Paradiso*, another journey altogether, unfolds Divinity as reflected in the order of the Dantesque cosmos. The beatific vision may be regarded as the center of the whole *Commedia*, because in Dante's living belief God is the clue to all our modes of life, including the life and form of his poem. Dante regarded himself as the heir of Aeneas and Paul; he certainly believed that he both saw and wrote in obedience to God. Yet at the same time he had a disabused and tender sense of mortal limitations, his own and the reader's; and he placed the vision of God outside the poem—an End and a Center which must remain ineffable. He explains clearly to Can Grande that he does not intend to explore heaven as the theologians try to do, speculatively, as it would be in itself. He reflects it, in successive aspects, in a changing human spirit, and only as it avails for the actual life—the nourishment and guidance—of that spirit. And the *Paradiso* also is based upon the journey-metaphor.

"But the *branch of philosophy* which regulates the work in its whole and in its parts," says Dante, explaining the *Comedy* to Can Grande, "is morals or ethics, because the whole was undertaken not for speculation but for practical results." Ethics and morals, and all didacticism, are in bad odor with us because we do not have much faith in our moralists. But when Dante says "moral philosophy" he means something like the natural history of the human psyche, the accumulated lore of its life. And when he says that this "philosophy" regulates the whole poem, including the *Paradiso*, he means that the underlying subject is always the modes of being and the destiny of the human psyche. The *Paradiso* presents it in relation to many reflections of its transcendent end; but it is the *Purgatorio* which explores the psyche itself—not in terms of its supernatural Goal, but in terms of its earthly existence.

It is therefore possible to read the *Purgatorio* both as a center of the whole *Commedia*, and as a poem with its own self-subsistent unity. The journey has its beginning in the *Antipurgatorio*, its center and turning-point in the evening of the second Day, its end in the *Paradiso Terrestre*. It is the visionary Fulfillment of the journey of *this* life, moving always, in many figures, toward what the soul may know of itself within its earthly destiny. It reflects Dante's own life, and by analogy, every man's.

The action of the *Purgatorio* has a natural source which is not too difficult to identify in one's own experience. After some deep fright, some nightmare-intuition of being nowhere, hope returns, and with hope the disquieting naïveté of the bare forked animal who needs to know who he is, where he is, and what he is trying to do. This need is, apparently, always with us. We may hear it in much of the murmuring of our innumerable radios, in popular music, in the vague complaining of the interminable soap-operas. We may detect it in ourselves whenever we are not too busy, sophisticated, or demoralized. The *Purgatorio* starts, after Hell, with this need; but Dante knew more about it than we do, and he found, in his time and place, the means to follow its promptings to the end.

Professor Maritain has spoken of the innocence and luck of Dante. The innocence—inseparable from courage, and deep to the point of genius—underlies both the terror and the triumphs of his journeys. His luck has to do with the moment of history in which he worked. Dante's Europe, Christian but full of ancient, Arabic, and Hebrew influences, must have seemed divided, deceptive, and confusing to those who lived in it. There were plenty of wars (to make us feel at home); poets in pursuit of their heretical inspirations; rulers making absolute claims; dissentions foreign and domestic. Dante himself was a displaced person, and he had plenty of reason to see the journeys of this life as lost, caught in the dead-ends of Hell. And yet, as Professor Curtius has recently shown, the culture formed then was to continue proliferating into the Renaissance and far beyond it. Some of its themes may still be heard well into the eighteenth century. The *Divine Comedy* reflects the path which Dante discovered through the actual confusion about him to the vision of an ideal order: it may be regarded as the epic of the discovery of Europe's traditional culture. This is especially true of the *Purgatorio*, the transitional canticle, the poem of initiations. Shelley's description of the *Commedia* as a bridge across time, joining the ancient and the modern world, fits the *Purgatorio* exactly. Or Eliot's dictum: "Dante and Shakespeare divide the modern world between them; there is no third."

It is strange that the *Divine Comedy* should have begun to be read again, after its eclipse during the period of the Enlightenment, just when the disappearance of the traditional culture was first sharply felt—with the revolutionary movements of the early romantics. Perhaps that is because the need for a way of life can only be felt with a depth comparable to Dante's, when no common way of life exists.

III

Dante has plainly indicated the main stages of the purgatorial journey, in the chronology of the ascent of the Mountain, and in the varied scenes of the climb. The first Day is spent in the foothills of the *Antipurgatorio*. The first night marks the mysterious transition to the realm of purgation proper, within the Gates. The second Day shows the ascent of the Mountain, painfully, under Virgil's guidance; and the second night marks another important change. During the third Day the ascent is easier, the scene of the climb more rich and exhilarating. The third night is spent on the threshold of Eden, and during the morning of the fourth Day, Eden, the *Paradiso Terrestre*, is explored. The literal narrative is clear; it recounts the ascent of a Mountain, from its rugged foothills to the meadowy plateau on its summit. But the distance figured in this climb is not spatial, but spiritual, like that between childhood and age. The movement which the reader is supposed to follow is double: that of the literal climb, and a movement of understanding, to which the developing inner life of Dante the Pilgrim is the clue.

One may start to enjoy the poetry of the *Purgatorio* immediately, but there is no short cut to understanding, no possibility of looking up the answers at the back of the book. It is true that Dante used many maps and blue-prints in building his great theater for this journey. There is a geographical plan, and an astronomical scheme governing the significant and elaborately worked-out chronology. There is a moral map, a Thomistic-Aristotelian classification of sins, with Pride at the bottom, nearest to Hell, and Lust at the top, nearest to Eden. The commentators have worked out most of these blueprints clearly, and their results are summarized in the excellent notes and appendices of the Temple Classics edition. But these abstract schemes have no more to do with what goes on in the poem than a road-map has to do with hitch-hiking to Chicago. Dante did not believe that the varied modes of human life could be "known" abstractly; the knowledge he seeks to convey is so close to home that it may actually avail to free and nourish the spirit. That is why, instead of writing a psychology, he dramatizes the acquisition of insight, carefully distinguishing between what he knows as author of the poem and what it takes, and means, to get knowledge.

Dante writes the poem as the record of a journey which he once took and now remembers. He writes in the first person; and yet the distinction between Dante speaking as the author, and Dante the Pilgrim, is fundamental to the whole structure. The author, when he reminds us of his existence, is outside the fictive world of the poem; the Pilgrim is the protagonist of the drama, the center of each scene. The author knows the whole story in advance, the Pilgrim meets everything freshly, for the first time. The two perspectives together produce a sort of stereoptical effect, that of an objective and partially mysterious reality. The shifting tensions between the two make the complex movement of the poem, and sustain its suspense. The Pilgrim is very much like one of Henry James's central intelligences, visible himself as a particular individual, yet revealing to the reader both the story and its meaning as he learns it. The Pilgrim's awareness is always moving toward the author's, but when they coincide, in the very strange and wonderful close of the *Paradiso Terrestre*, all narrative movement, and all growth of understanding, cease. While the poem unfolds, the Pilgrim's awareness is the moving center of the composition.

Dante explained to Can Grande how his poem was to be read and understood. "The exposition of the letter," he wrote, "is nought else than the development of the form." By the *letter* he meant the literal fiction of the journeys to the other world, all that the Pilgrim sees and feels and hears there. By the *development of the form* he meant that musical or dramatic unfolding which I tried to describe above: the drama of the Pilgrim's growing understanding. It has not, I think, been sufficiently noticed how strongly Dante puts his prescription for interpreting his poem: the exposition (or interpretation) *is* the development of the form—not any aspect of the structure which may be abstracted and considered as a static scheme, but the shifting life of the growing soul itself, imitated in the ceaseless movement of the *terza rima*.

The plan of these studies is intended to follow Dante's prescription as I understand it. Each phase of the journey—from childhood to age, or from innocence to natural sanctity—has its own irreducible significance, its own mode of understanding, which is imitated in the poem itself. The four parts of the book are devoted to the four Days of the journey. The titles

I have used for the four Days are intended to suggest the nature of the drama, always a struggle for freedom and understanding, but going on in a different way in each phase of growth. It is necessary to linger over each one, because they are so different from each other.

IV

Dante announces the theme of the whole *Purgatorio*, with his usual decision, in the opening chords of the very first canto:

> Per correr miglior acqua alza le vele
> omai la navicella del mio ingegno,
> che lascia retro a sè mar sì crudele.

> (To run over better waters now hoists sail
> the little bark of my native talent,
> which leaves behind it a sea so cruel.)

The search for the better describes the action, the movement-of-spirit, of the whole poem. But the metaphor of the ocean voyage is not connected with the journey up the Mountain. Dante is speaking as author, outside the fictive world of the *Purgatorio*, of a journey which is neither that of this life, nor that of Hell, but the hope-inspired journey of the *making* of this canticle:

> E canterò di quel secondo regno
> dove l'umano spirito si purga,
> e di salire al ciel diventa degno.

> (And I shall sing of that second kingdom
> wherein the human spirit is made clean,
> becoming worthy to ascend to heaven.)

He goes on (lines 7-13) to bid dead poetry, the poetry of the ancient world, to rise again to help him.

We feel the lift of the ocean-voyage through the whole

passage, as we do in the more triumphant use of that metaphor in the second canto of the *Paradiso*, which I quoted above. We may also remember the ocean-music of Ulysses' superb narrative of his foolish flight into these realms (Inferno xxvi)—"to seek virtue and knowledge," as he told his followers. This is one of several echoes of Ulysses' voyage in the first canto, and no doubt Dante wishes to suggest an analogy between Ulysses' motive and the aspiration which moves him to poetry here. But he does not offer explanations of these relationships. We know that the Pilgrim, leaving Ulysses, descended to the bottom, and then found that his descent had mysteriously turned into a climb upward. We know that Ulysses was wrecked on a Mountain which he had not foreseen. The aspiration of this canticle is like Ulysses' but reborn beyond his confines. But it would be a mistake to try to connect these voyages literally: they are different, and very Dantesque, uses of the journey-metaphor, each with its own relation to the journey of this life.

In line 13 we suddenly find ourselves in this realm, at the beginning of this journey, with the Pilgrim, weak after Hell, where dawn finds him on the beach:

> Dolce color d'oriental zaffiro,
>   che s'accoglieva nel sereno aspetto
>   dell'aer puro infino al primo giro,
> agli occhi miei ricominciò diletto,
>   tosto ch'i'uscii fuor dell'aura morta,
>   che m'avea contristati gli occhi e il petto.

> (The tender color of the eastern sapphire,
>   which was appearing in the tranquil height
>   of pure air, as far as to the first gyre,
> restored to my eyes once more their delight,
>   as soon as I emerged from the dead air
>   which had so saddened both my eyes and heart.)

The author, outside the poem, speaks with a sense of its

vast scope, its difference from life itself, and its varied but related themes of journeying. But the Pilgrim can only see the comforting return of an earthly dawn. The distance between them suggests the distance we have to go, and the childlike state of being with which *this* journey begins.

઒ CHAPTER 2. BEFORE
UNDERSTANDING

THE *Antipurgatorio*, Cantos I-VIII, is devoted to the first Day in the new realm. It is the prologue to the drama of spiritual growth which begins, reaches its climax, and comes to its end during the second and third Days; and it corresponds to the *Paradiso Terrestre*, another set-piece, placed, like the epiphany of a Sophoclean tragedy, at the end of the action.

I observed in the last chapter that Dante the Pilgrim, when he first emerges from Hell (Canto I, line 13) is very far from understanding what Dante the author does. The author, in his direct address to the reader, and in his invocation, suggests the epic scope of the journey to follow. But the Pilgrim is really there, all defenceless, on the beach. The beauty of earth restores the delight of the heart and the senses; it reaches him with the intimacy of childhood memory, but he does not understand what it could (and will) mean to him. During the whole first Day of wandering he will see everything in this way, deeply but without understanding.

Because the *Antipurgatorio* presents a mode of experience preceding understanding and moral, conscious effort, it is difficult to get on a first reading, unless one knows what to look for. This effect, of course, is intended: Dante wishes the reader to feel the force of an aspiration which cannot effectuate itself, the poetry of our most primitive awareness of the earthly scene. The *Antipurgatorio* is best reread; and for that reason I do not propose to study any of it in detail, but to offer a few general observations on the scene and the action of the first Day as a whole.

We are told explicitly that the spirits we meet in this realm died, for one reason or another, outside the Church; through blind chance, or others' malice, or some dilatoriness of their own. Thus they all lost, or failed to find their way; yet they have not lost the good of the intellect, they are not fixed

· 14 ·

eternally in some depraved mode of being, like those in Hell. They still have the potentialities of sane growth, if they could only discover how to begin. Their plight is thus like that of the human creature in general when deprived of a living tradition; or like that of every child or young person who has not yet found himself in his world. Throughout the *Antipurgatorio* there runs the lyric of this unfulfilled aspiration, and I shall have something to say of it in the next chapter. Here I shall point out the nature of the visible scene, at the foot of the Mountain; of the stories we hear there; and, first of all, of the Pilgrim's feelings and inchoate perceptions, the center of the composition.

The Pilgrim, from the time he comes to himself after Hell, until he sleeps at the end of the first Day, "sees as a child and understands as a child," as Saint Paul puts it. He is not literally a child, but thirty-three years old; moreover he is well-read in literature, philosophy, history, and theology, and thoroughly instructed in the doctrines and practice of the medieval Church. But after the vision of Hell his formal knowledge avails him little. He has to make a new beginning; and in his candor, obedience to the immediate impression, and freedom of feeling, he is like a child. The life of his spirit is well described in the lines which Marco Lombardo uses for the human spirit before the world confuses and divides it (Canto xvi, line 88):

> l'anima semplicetta, che sa nulla,
>   salvo che, mossa da lieto fattore,
>   volentier torna a ciò che la trastulla.

> (the small and simple soul, who knows nothing,
>   except that, moved by a joyous maker,
>   she turns in willingness to what is pleasing.)

But Marco's vision belongs to another realm of experience: the Pilgrim at this point is, but cannot grasp, the simple soul. What the Pilgrim sees, looking outward, is the natural world as the eye of innocence perceives it. We shall learn from Statius (in Canto xxi, line 40 ff.) that here, below the gates of purgatory proper, earthly weather prevails. There is no more to guide us here than there would be in a new country, where dawn, noon, and dusk are vaguely familiar, but no road appears, no sign to show the way. Thus the scene itself defines the state of the Pilgrim and of those he meets. Even Virgil shares that state, for though he guides the Pilgrim as well as he can, he is with him, sees what he sees, and can do no more until the "scene" changes. But he can tell the Pilgrim and the reader how to take this experience (Canto iii, line 37):

> State contenti, umana gente, al *quia*:
>> chè, se potuto aveste veder tutto,
>> mestier non era partorir Maria;
> e disiar vedeste senza frutto
>> tai, che sarebbe lor disio quetato,
>> ch'eternalmente è dato lor per lutto.
> Io dico d'Aristotele e di Plato
>> e di molti altri.

> (Be satisfied, you human race, with *quia*:
>> Had you been able to see everything
>> there would have been no need for Mary's labor;
> and you have seen the fruitless hungering
>> of those whose appetite would have been sated,
>> which now is given them as eternal grieving.
> I speak of Aristotle here, and Plato,
>> and many others.)

Virgil means that the human mind must accept the "what" of the world in which it finds itself, without demanding to know the "why," which is a matter of faith and of the Revelation which emerged from Mary's labor. The general principle holds, in many subtle ways, to the top of the Mountain. But it has special force here. We must accept the new realm literally, as the necessary preliminary to transcending it.

All the little episodes of the first Day, and all the life-histories we hear, are in the sensitive, restrained style which Virgil's advice suggests. Consider, for example, the tentative movement of the spirits in Canto III, line 79:

> Come le pecorelle escon del chiuso
>   ad una, a due, a tre, e l'altre stanno
>   timidette atterrando l'occhio e il muso;
> e ciò che fa la prima, e l'altre fanno,
>   addossandosi a lei s'ella s'arresta,
>   semplici e quete, e lo'mperchè non sanno:
> sì vid'io movere a venir la testa
>   di quella mandria fortunata allotta,
>   pudica in faccia, e nell'andare onesta.

> (Just as sheep come out of their enclosure
>   singly, in twos, in threes, while the rest huddle
>   timid, eyes and nose to the ground before them;
> and what the first one does the others follow,
>   jostling against her if she come to pause there,
>   knowing no reason, placable and callow:
> so I saw then, moving to come forward,
>   him who was leader of that fortunate flock,
>   candid in his slow steps, in his face timid.)

Manfred tells us (Canto III, line 130) of his bones, washed by the rain, and lets the picture stand for a fate he does not fathom. Belacqua, under the shade of his rock (Canto IV, line 102) knows only that he can know and do nothing here. In Canto V, the narratives of Jacopo del Cassero, Buonconte da Montefeltro, and La Pia, which are joined in the image of the down-flowing river, owe much of their force and beauty to the fact that the narrators explain nothing. They give the mysterious facts of their earthly destiny, beyond which they cannot see.

Virgil himself, as I observed, is, at the moment, in the

Antipurgatorio with us, and when he explains his condition to Sordello (Canto VII, line 25) he does so in such a way as to bring out the analogy between his state of eternal exile and this more hopeful realm of being:

> Non per far, ma per non far ho perduto
> di veder l'alto Sol che tu disiri,
> e che fu tardi da me conosciuto.

> (Not through doing, through what I did not do
> I lost the vision of the Sun you long for,
> and whom, too tardily, I came to know.)

He proceeds to describe the Castle of the Pagan Sages where he has his timeless dwelling-place. The Pilgrim had seen it, in Limbo, near the beginning of the whole journey; and we know it as the place of those who live "in desire but without hope." This realm *has* hope, but, like Limbo, it lacks the vision it desires. Virgil knows the *Antipurgatorio*, therefore, by sympathy, but with the sad clarity of those who have come to the end of their development. That is why he plays the role of parent to the Pilgrim, washing his face, girding him with a rush, leading and encouraging him as he would a child.

Virgil guides the Pilgrim, but the Pilgrim guides us; and what happens to him, if one can learn to see it, shows the movement of the whole first Day. In general, this first Day may be called a "Pathos," to distinguish it from the second Day, which is a "drama of ethical motivation," as Aristotle would have said. The Pilgrim, because he understands so little, does not proceed by will, he suffers; the course of his inner life is a rise and fall of feeling.

In the first canto he absorbs the scene by the beach, while Virgil prepares him for the journey. In the second canto he begins to cover the physical distance he will have to go, and meets the first of the spirits who are lost here. He is simply obedient, in this wandering: to Virgil, and to what he sees and hears; dawdling in the enjoyment of Casella's song (Canto III, line 115), then fleeing with him like frightened pigeons, or (line 132) like one who goes and does not know where he will come out. In Canto IV he must make a steep climb, but even this is done by feeling rather than by will, or according to a conscious purpose: "with the swift wings and with the feathers of great desire," as we read in line 28. This is the first indication that the feeling which has moved him is building to a climax. This feeling in the beginning was brief pleasure in the dawn, or in the song, and homesickness, the sense of distance. Now it grows more intense, and in Canto V, in the river-image which accompanies the narrative of Buonconte, we hear it as a lament for all that the human must suffer (line 115):

> Indi la valle, come il dì fu spento,
>> da Pratomagno al gran giogo coperse
>> di nebbia, e il ciel di sopra fece intento
> sì che il pregno aere in acqua si converse:
>> la pioggia cadde, ed ai fossati venne
>> di lei ciò che la terra non sofferse;
> e come a' rivi grandi si convenne,
>> ver lo fiume real tanto veloce
>> si ruinò, che nulla la ritenne.

> (Then all that valley, when the day was done,
>> he clouded over, from the mountain summit
>> to Pratomagno; the sky hung low above
> until the pregnant air was turned to water:
>> the rain came down, into the ditches flowed
>> all of the waters the earth could not suffer;
> converging in great torrents then, they poured
>> with such a swift rush toward the royal stream
>> as nothing, in its downward course, could hold.)

The image of the down-rushing river was first suggested in Canto III. It is connected with many rivers throughout the

Commedia. Here, just before the climax and turning-point of the pathos of the first Day, it not only holds together the narratives of those who were slain before repentance, as I observed above; it also expresses the compulsions of passion and of external fate which the Pilgrim feels after all he has seen. Its stormy imagery and its headlong rhythm are re-sumed and intensified in Dante's outburst over the condition of his native Italy (Canto vi, line 76 ff.):

> Ahi serva Italia, di dolore ostello,
> > nave senza nocchiero in gran tempesta,
> > non donna di provincie, ma bordello!

> (Ah servile Italy, ah dolor's hostel!
> > ship without a pilot in a great storm,
> > no mistress of your provinces, but brothel!)

The great tirade, a mixture of grief and anger over the des-tiny of Italy, continues for seventy-five lines. Dante utters it in his own voice, as author, as though he had momentarily despaired of his poem-making, just as the Pilgrim almost despairs of his journey. The immediate effect is to break the texture of the fictive narrative; but the next moment (when we remember the other perspective) we are back in the poem again, with a deeper sense of its meaning for the helplessness of actual human life.

The lament over Italy is the climax of that movement of feeling which governs the whole first Day; and immediately after it this feeling begins to quiet down again into some-thing like patience. Day is declining (Canto vii, line 43), and, as Sordello explains, no one can travel upward on the Mountain during the dark hours. Sordello guides them to a good place to spend the night, the beautiful valley where the rulers who were negligent on earth pause and suffer their dilatoriness as nostalgia. While we are in this valley, night descends, and the movement of the first Day ends quietly.

The closing sequence is the best place in which to study

the delicately-perceived state of being, the childlike mode of the inner life, of the first Day. It is there that the Pilgrim accepts his own unsatisfied aspiration, and the beautiful, but mysterious earthly scene which it is given to him to see. From the point of view of the plot of the whole journey, one may say that, in Canto VIII, we see the Pilgrim accepting the vast distance between his situation and what he longs to see. It is the distance which the attentive reader felt in the first canto, between the awareness of the Pilgrim on the beach, and the awareness of the author, who knows that change and growing enlightenment are to come.

Because the *Antipurgatorio* is a pathos, its movement is musical or lyric. One of the best ways to get its meaning is to listen for the song which underlies it, and which may be heard, sometimes more clearly, sometimes less, in the detail of the verse. In the next chapter I shall make some observations on the lyric of the *Antipurgatorio*, especially as it comes out in the eighth canto.

ɜ❧ CHAPTER 3. THE FINE VEIL OF POETRY

O voi, che avete gl'intelletti sani,
    mirate la dottrina, che s'asconde
    sotto il velame degli versi strani!

(O all of you whose intellects are sane,
    turn your eyes now to the knowledge hidden
    under the veil of verse, which is so strange!)
                        —*Inferno*, Canto ɪx, lines 61-63

Mʀ. T. S. Eʟɪoᴛ, in his book on Dante which has done so much to lead readers of English to the *Commedia*, advises us to begin "with the poetry." He means by "poetry" the verses themselves which, even on a first reading, may give immediate pleasure. And he quotes many passages which any reader who is fairly familiar with modern lyric verse will recognize as singularly beautiful. In the last chapter I considered, not the "poetry" of the *Antipurgatorio*, but its dramatic form and its characterizations. But I believe that Mr. Eliot's advice is good. We must start to enjoy Dante by recognizing effects like those of the poetry we know, and our sense of poetry is based on the modern lyric. Moreover, Dante certainly intended to lead the reader into his complex composition through the pleasures of poetry in this sense. He expects us to start with "the Letter," by which he means the literal fiction of the journey beyond the grave; and it is the imagery and the music of his verses which give us the experience of the successive scenes which the Pilgrim enters in that spirit-world.

Mr. Eliot's advice is especially good in the reading of the *Antipurgatorio*. I have called it a Pathos, or drama of pathetic motivation. I have also pointed out that in this realm the Pilgrim sees and feels with that directness and subtlety which we associate with childhood and its "intimations of immortality," but without intellectual understanding. This mode of awareness has been prized above all, by lyric poets, since the early romantics; they think of it as the source of poetry itself, as distinguished from philosophy, science, and all varieties of conceptual thought. When the Pilgrim is most "aware," in the *Antipurgatorio*, it is in this way that he is aware; and because he does not change or break through into new regions, he is always aware of the same "distant" or homesick scene. You may say that the *Antipurgatorio* contains a lyric of vague aspiration, very close to that of modern poetry, and that this lyric emerges from the singularly coherent imagery of the whole wandering first Day, and reaches its end in Canto VIII, the eve of change.

It is at those moments when the Pilgrim can look about him, question his deepest feeling, and sense his whole situation, that the lyric comes through most clearly. We hear it in Canto I, line 118:

> Noi andavam per lo solingo piano,
>> com'uom che torna a la perduta strada,
>> che infino ad essa gli par ire in vano.

> (We were walking along the lonely plain
>> like one who turns back to the road he lost
>> and, till he reach it, seems to walk in vain.)

A more suggestive variation of this image is in Canto II, line 10:

> Noi eravam lunghesso il mare ancora,
>> come gente che pensa suo cammino,
>> che va col core, e col corpo dimora.

> (We were still along the edge of the sea,
>> like those who have the road ahead in mind;
>> who move in spirit, and in body stay.)

A similar distance and nostalgia is expressed by Virgil

(Canto III, line 25) in the terms he finds to describe his own ghostly being:

> Vespero è già colà, dov'è sepolto
> lo corpo, dentro al quale io facea ombra.

> (It is now evening, there where lies interred
> the body, wherein I once made shadow.)

It is in the image of the flooded river, carrying the body it knows not where (Canto v), that this "lyric of aspiration" is at once most despairing and most intense, as I mentioned in the last chapter.

In Canto VIII, as the Pilgrim quiets down for the evening, and lends ear to his day's experiences and their possible meanings, this lyric is epitomized and concluded. Canto VIII, line 1:

> Era già l'ora che volge il disio
> ai naviganti, e intenerisce il core
> lo dì ch'han detto ai dolci amici addio;
> e che lo nuovo peregrin d'amore
> punge, se ode squilla di lontano,
> che paia il giorno pianger che si more:
> quand'io incomminciai a render vano
> l'udire, ed a mirare una dell'alme
> surta, che l'ascoltar chiedea con mano.

> (It was the hour which turns back the desires
> of seafarers, and makes the spirit tender
> that day they told their well-loved friends good-bye;
> hour when love will sting the new pilgrim
> if he hear, from far away, bells ringing,
> a lament, it seems, for the day's ending:
> when I began to annul my sense of hearing
> and gaze at one of the spirits, who arose,
> and with a gesture of his hand craved listening.)

The modern reader of this passage can hardly fail to be reminded of a great deal of nineteenth-century homesickness; the far-off traveller, the evening, the distant bells, are almost too familiar. There is no doubt, I think, that Dante means to give us that "feeling" which we know so well. At the same time, the passage has the unique quality we call *Dantesque*, and that comes from the accuracy with which this inarticulate response of the inner being is defined. The literal scene with its sounds is only the signal for love (apparently from without) to pierce the Pilgrim. And he listens for it, not with the ear of the flesh, but with the whole being; he "looks" for something which is to be perceptible through the dusky scene around him. This is one of the many places in which Dante uses the shift from one physical sense to another to suggest a focus of attention which is not to be defined as sight, hearing, or any other single sense. He wants us to be poised, thus all attentive, for some clue to the meaning of the love that pierces the Pilgrim: is it frightening or comforting? Good or evil?

The clue which appears is that pair of green-feathered messengers of heaven who come winging through the evening air and alight, one on either side of the valley. It is not difficult to discover that they represent that "love" which prevails in the whole realm of purgation, the divine grace, the unearned gift, which prevents the Pilgrim from taking the wrong path until he reaches the *Paradiso Terrestre*. For the *Purgatorio* shows *one* view of human destiny, man as mysteriously capable—capable beyond what he can understand— of sane growth. The messengers' immediate errand, however, is to frighten away the snake, ancient and familiar sign of that other version of love, the human potentiality of evil, which also appears whenever darkness begins to fall and the moral will is in abeyance. The Pilgrim, poised here without will or intellectual grasp, is vaguely aware of the various meanings of his emotion and of the evening scene before him.

It is the highest point of awareness which the Pilgrim reaches in the *Antipurgatorio*, and Dante marks it by one of his author's interpolations (line 19):

> Aguzza qui, lettor, ben gli occhi al vero,
> che il velo è ora ben tanto sottile,
> certo, che il trapassar entro è leggiero.

> (Sharpen your eyes toward the truth here, reader,
> for now what veils it is become so fine
> that, surely, to pass through it would be easy.)

It is very much like the interpolation quoted at the head of this chapter, which also reminds the reader of the meaning behind the immediate poetic awareness, the mysterious grace which makes the whole journey possible. Its effect is to break the "veil of the verses," and thus the literal course of the narrative. We see that behind the fictive world of the dead which the verses present (what Dante in his *Letter to Can Grande* calls "the first subject") there is the meaning (which Dante calls "the second subject") that the whole poem has for human life in the actual world, as we know it here below. We are reminded that there is an analogy between some of our efforts to see meaning in our world, and the efforts of the Pilgrim to understand what he sees and feels on the evening of the first Day.

The Pilgrim himself does not have the notes of the commentators, and he does not make the deductions which the reader may make; and after the interpolated tercet, Dante returns us to the Pilgrim. For him, the valley and the evening, and even the messengers of heaven, speak only like one of Wordsworth's calm evenings; or like Baudelaire's forest of symbols, through which man passes with an odd sense of familiarity, but without quite grasping the meaning. This is one of the themes which recurs in many forms in European lyric poetry since the early romantics. Eliot uses it in many subtle variations in the *Four Quartets*. Dante himself presents the poetry of many scenes of felt but undeclared significance; the semi-transparent "veil" is always there, at the edge of whatever region we are in.

After the moment of pause with which the canto opens, the Pilgrim turns from the wide sense of his whole situation, to talk with some of the spirits who are waiting here with him. It is a movement, not of enquiry, nor of effort to pierce the veil, but of acceptance and realization. The words of Nino de' Visconti convey this acceptance with many rich overtones and echoing implications (line 67):

> Poi volto a me: "Per quel singular grado,
>   che tu dei a colui, che sì nasconde
>   lo suo primo perchè, che non gli è guado,
> quando sarai di là dalle larghe onde,
>   di' a Giovanna mia, che per me chiami
>   là dove agl'innocenti si risponde.

> (Then turning toward me: "By that special favor
>   you owe to him who keeps so deeply covered
>   his final purpose, that there is no way there,
> When you shall be beyond the wide water,
>   tell my Giovanna to appeal for me,
>   there where the innocent receive an answer.)

The passage is full of the lyric theme of "distance" in many forms: between Nino and his remembered Giovanna, between this "world" and the real world, between our counsels and the counsels of God. But the distance is patiently accepted, and accompanied by a curious tenderness of personal relationships: between Nino and his remembered daughter, and between Nino and Dante, whom he sees only briefly. These relationships, which mean so much and so little, are very much like those in Chekhov's second acts, as I have pointed out in another context. And so is the movement of the canto as a whole, from the wide but inchoate awareness of the beginning, to the descent of darkness near the end, when the stars come out. The stars—"three torches," as the Pilgrim calls them—play the role of Faith, Hope, and Charity in Dante's symbolic scheme, appearing whenever darkness makes it impossible to see ahead and move ahead. But the Pilgrim here knows them only as stars which have replaced the four he saw, near dawn, at the beginning of his day's journey.

Because the Pilgrim does not essentially change in the *Antipurgatorio*, or break through into other regions, the scene is bounded by the same lyric awareness during the whole Day, from dawn to the descent of night. And for that reason, it is the lyric effects which we hear, from time to time, throughout the eight cantos, that most directly present that childlike mode of being which Dante wished to show. But the narrative is interrupted from time to time by explanations which Virgil or one of the spirits gives, or which the author interpolates; and they remind us that this first Day is merely the prelude to a more conscious drama to follow.

Some of the explanations and comments in the *Antipurgatorio* hint at the nature of the childlike lyric awareness which bounds it, suggesting its limitations and perils. In the second canto, for example (line 112), we see the Pilgrim and the shadowy Casella caught in the enjoyment of Casella's song, a setting of Dante's own *canzone*:

> "*Amor che nella mente mi ragiona,*"
>   cominciò egli allor sì dolcemente,
>   che la dolcezza ancor dentro mi suona.
> Lo mio maestro ed io e quella gente
>   ch'eran con lui parevan sì contenti,
>   come a nessun toccasse altro la mente.

> ("*Love that in my mind discourses to me,*"
>   the spirit so sweetly thereupon commenced,
>   that still I hear the sweetness sound within me.
> My Master then and I and all the rest
>   who were with him, showed forth such happiness
>   as though our minds played upon nothing else.)

Upon which Cato scolds them for laziness and chases them away. In Canto IV, beginning with the first line, there is a very significant interpolation by the author on the psychology of *any* pleasure (or pain) which may hold the soul, depriving it of its freedom of response through the very depth of the immediate impression. And there is the explicit statement in Canto VIII which I quoted above, that the poetry is a "veil" which we must see *through* to reach the truth behind it.

Such hints and brief statements as these show that Dante regarded the childlike poetic awareness, the absorbed listening with the inner ear, as only one recurrent moment in the growth of the soul; and that he intended to get lyric effects only from time to time, even in the *Antipurgatorio*. Croce, in his reading of the *Commedia*, accurately perceived that: we hear "poetry," in the sense of the modern lyric poetry, only from time to time. Croce proceeded to reject all the rest as dead sign-language, mere allegorizing in an outworn convention. Croce's view of the *Commedia* is now, I think, generally regarded as inadequate. But because he is so consistent, pushing to its logical conclusion the attempt to read the *Commedia* according to modern notions of poetry, he reveals the perils of this method very clearly. Dante is master of a lyric style, and thoroughly understands its sources and its pleasures and insights; but in writing the *Commedia* he was limited neither by the *mystique* nor by the poetics of our modern poetry.

Because the *Antipurgatorio* is the place of vague beginnings, of hopeful responses, and of problems sensed but not solved, it should be reread in the light of the whole canticle. But the plan of these studies is to follow as closely as possible Dante's own order of exposition or interpretation. And the next step is to consider the Pilgrim's passage into Purgatory proper, the more and more conscious efforts of the second Day.

ঌ CHAPTER 4. CANTO IX: THE PROPHETIC FIRST NIGHT

> che or sì or no s'intendon le parole.
> (When now the words are clear, and now are not.)
> —Canto ix, line 145.

IN CANTO IX the childlike Pilgrim of the first eight cantos goes to sleep in the last valley of the *Antipurgatorio*, dreams, and wakes in the bright sunshine of a new day in a new place: before the ancient gates of Purgatory proper. This is his first mutation, or break-through into a wider mode of awareness. Canto ix reveals this mysterious passage in many ways, foreshadowing the stages of the journey all the way to the top of the Mountain. It is a good place to pause and attempt a more careful reading, for this canto may show a great deal about the Pilgrim's half-conscious growth, and about the author's methods of composition.

The canto begins with a single smooth sentence of twelve lines, which suggests both the passage of night over our heads, and the Pilgrim's weary sinking to sleep:

> La concubina di Titone antico
>   già s'imbiancava al balco d'oriente,
>   fuor delle braccia del suo dolce amico;
> di gemme la sua fronte era lucente,
>   poste in figura del freddo animale,
>   che con la coda percote la gente;
> e la notte de' passi, con che sale,
>   fatti avea due nel loco ov'eravamo,
>   e il terzo già chinava in giuso l'ale;
> quand'io, che meco avea di quel d'Adamo,
>   vinto dal sonno, in su l'erba inchinai
>   ove già tutti e cinque sedevamo.

(The concubine of Tithonous the ancient
  was growing white on eastern parapet,
    as she came forth from her sweet friend's embraces;
her forehead was alight with shine of gems
  fixed in the figure of that cold live thing
    which with its flickering tail transfixes men;
and night, upon the stairway of her climbing,
  had mounted twice, there where we then tarried,
    and for the third her wings was down-inclining,
when I, who had in me somewhat of Adam,
  sank overcome by sleep upon the lawn,
    in that place where all five of us had rested.)

The position of the stars shows the hour. The moon's aurora
is on the eastern horizon, where the constellation of Scorpio
glitters as though upon a white forehead. The aurora of the
moon is a false dawn, hence a "concubine." The associations
are with the myths and superstitions of pagan antiquity, the
hard but majestic world of unredeemed nature. The Pilgrim
yields to the weight of body and to the logic and vast regu-
larity of the movements of the heavens, like a child going
to sleep in a well-ordered household. The only association
with the Christian tradition in this passage is that of *Adamo*,
significantly rhymed with *sedevamo*.

The whole passage is a poetic evocation of night as Sordello had predicted it in Canto vii, line 52. The darkness
paralyzes the will, and therefore one cannot climb upward,
though one might descend as though by gravitation back
down the Mountain, toward that dead center we passed at
the bottom of Hell. In all of the nights this possibility is
suggested; sleep, the sign of our bodily being, our old Adam,
is an image of death. But when this mortal weakness is
obediently accepted, the sleeping spirit is in a sense freed for
another mode of life; and that is presented in the next six
lines, dawn on the Mountain and in the sleeper:

Nell'ora che comincia i tristi lai
la rondinella presso alla mattina,
forse a memoria de'suoi primi guai,
e che la mente nostra, peregrina
più dalla carne e men da'pensier presa,
alle sue vision quasi è divina:

(At the hour when begins the sad song
which the swallow twitters near to morning,
perhaps in memory of her first wrong,
and when our pilgrim spirit, wandering
far from the body and the prison of thought
is, in her visions, very near foreknowing:)

The swallow is Philomela. According to the story as Dante
used it, Philomela was raped by Tereus, the husband of
Procne, who was Philomela's sister. Tereus cut out Philomela's tongue, but she was able to tell Procne of her wrong
by means of a tapestry she wove; and Procne then took
vengeance on Tereus by serving him his son's flesh in a
covered dish. When Tereus discovered what he had eaten, he
pursued the sisters to kill them; but the god had pity, changing Procne into a nightingale and Philomela into a swallow.
Such are the primal sufferings, the *primi guai* which we still
hear in the wordless voices of the swallows when they wake
near dawn.

The myth-making childhood of the race, the feel of early
morning, the ancient plaint of nature in the bird-sounds, are
poetically or imaginatively fused in this passage. The suggested significance of this moment and this scene is what the
childlike sleeper himself might sense; and as in the night-
sequence, the scene leads to the Pilgrim's state of awareness.

In the second tercet the nature of the sleeper's awareness
is exactly specified: he is as free as mortals ever get from the
limitations of the flesh, and also from the confinement of
"thought," by which I think Dante means the concepts and

the logical concatenations of the discursive reason. He is aware by means of visions, which are *almost* truly divinatory. This visionary state is akin to that "poetic awareness" which the Pilgrim had, at various moments, during the preceding day, and which we looked at in the last chapter. Here it is also associated with the poetry of the race, the heritage of myth. The whole passage is allusive, in a manner akin to the late work of Joyce, Pound, and Eliot. By means of allusion, a timeless or recurrent mode of human awareness is suggested.

But the six lines are merely introductory to the dream, which is both a dream as we know dreams, and a vision containing truth. In the latter aspect, the dream which follows is very much like the rainbow-colored shows and pageants which we shall see in the *Paradiso Terrestre*: true, but impermeable to conscious understanding. The dream follows without a break:

> in sogno mi parea veder sospesa
> un'aquila nel ciel con penne d'oro
> con l'ali aperte, ed a calare intesa.
> Ed esser mi parea là dove foro
> abbandonati i suoi da Ganimede,
> quando fu ratto al sommo consistoro.
> Fra me pensava: "Forse questa fiede
> pur qui per uso, e forse d'altro loco
> disdegna di portarne suso in piede."

> (in dream I seemed to see an eagle, taut
> on his spread feathers in the sky above me,
> poised there on wings of gold, intent to drop.
> And I was in that place, it seemed to me,
> where Ganymede abandoned his companions,
> when he was snatched to the high consistory.
> I thought within me: "Only in this region,
> perhaps, he strikes, and elsewhere he disdains
> to seize and lift one upward in his talons.")

The account of the dream, as it struck the Pilgrim, continues through line 42, when the Pilgrim wakes. The dream itself wakes the dreamer; and there is no telling how many waking minutes it occupies. The eagle swoops and lifts the Pilgrim up to the fiery sphere in which they burn together. The burning wakes the dreamer, and as he wakes his surprise is associated with that of Achilles; whose mother, the sea-nymph Thetis, lifted him up from among his enemies, while he slept, and carried him to safety. The effect of the dream-passage, as one reads it, is like that of the dreams we know: there is some sort of passage, of being carried; but the place, the people, and the purpose shift and fuse as we watch. Our sensations are ambivalent also: we are honored, terrified, reassured, and burned to the point where the whole vision breaks, we wake, and the actual world comes back.

The movement of the canto from dreaming to waking, where the dream will be explained to the Pilgrim in a certain way, does not cease. But if one stops to consider the static structure of the dream-passage, and its place in the predesigned framework of the whole *Purgatorio*, one learns that a very extensive scale of meaning has been built into it.

At the top of this scale, beyond the understanding of Pilgrim or reader at this point, are the meanings of the Eagle in Dante's symbolic scheme. The useful notes in the Temple Classics edition refer us to the Eagle of the medieval Bestiaries, who like the Phoenix is perpetually burned and renewed, and so stands for baptismal regeneration. These notes also connect the Eagle with the Roman Empire, and so with Virgil and the pagan moral and intellectual virtues; and with the secular institutions of government that safeguard justice. Other commentators tell us confidently that the Eagle also stands for illuminating grace. The question is surrounded by erudite disputes which I am not qualified to enter. Suffice it (for my purposes) to say that the Eagle suggests secular, ecclesiastical, and divine assistance—"Grace" (the unearned gift) which may come in many ways—and which, at crucial moments, is needed for the growth of the spirit. In Dante's own plan of interpretation, these matters will be explored in many contexts farther up the Mountain, when the relations of Church and State, of tradition and individual experience, of pagan and Christian culture, are slowly sorted out by the Pilgrim and his guides.

In the center of the scale of meanings of the dream are those which the dreamer, with his non-rational but poetic and mythopoeic awareness, is groping for. He feels an analogy between what is happening to him and what happened to Ganymede, the beautiful shepherd whom Jove fell in love with and kidnapped. But as he wakes another analogy with a myth is suggested, that of Achilles borne away by his mother, not to be raped but to be saved. This analogy is closer than the first one to the literal facts of the nocturnal passage which the Pilgrim will learn when he wakes. The whole dream, near the end of the night, represents the end of a process of inner clarification. In this Dante confirms a very ancient tradition, that the dreams we have nearest the morning are the most true; and he anticipates Freud, who reaches the same conclusion. But Freud (unlike Jung) would not agree that the "truth" of morning dreams is that of a recurrent, and thus in a sense timeless mode of human experience; he sees them as revealing only the emotional state of the individual dreamer.

At the "bottom" of the dream's scale of meanings, Dante seems to be aware of the kind of truth Freud likes. The swooping bird, the ascent, and the burning-together, have erotic connotations which would have delighted Freud if he had read this passage attentively. He would have said, perhaps, that they show that the dreamer's suppressed desires were infantile, or "polymorphous-perverse," in his unpleasing phrase. I am sure Dante meant the erotic connotations, for the whole *Purgatorio* may be regarded as the epic of the transformations of love. And he also knew that the Pilgrim's love was unformed and childish at this point; the eroticism of the next dream (Canto XIX) is much more conscious, formed, and "adult." He knew that what the dreamer could grasp in his visions of this experience (itself a standard moment of psychic growth) was colored and limited by his emotional-moral state. Both mythic analogues suggest the passivity of childhood. But Dante attaches more weight to the Pilgrim's inarticulate, visionary effort for wider understanding than he does to his emotional state at that moment; for it is partly by means of this effort (the response to what happens *to* him) that his love, or "libido," will be transformed and widened.

In the next passage (line 43) we see the Pilgrim wake from his terrible and wonderful dream:

> Da lato m'era solo il mio conforto,
>   e il sole er'alto già più che due ore,
>   e il viso m'era alla marina torto.

> (Only my comfort was there beside me,
>   the sun already more than two hours high,
>   and my gaze in the direction of the sea.)

This waking, with its mixture of relief and deflation, suggests a familiar experience. After going to sleep with an unsolved problem and spending a night of hope, fear, and half-formed insights, the daylight world comes back; but now it "looks different." The insoluble problem of the night before, whether it be one of tangled personal relationships, or an intellectual problem like those of artists, mathematicians, and scientific investigators, has been turned around during the night by some force which we do not understand. It may or may not be solved, but it appears in a new light; and now we can at least see how to work on it with the pedestrian efforts of the waking, rational mind. Modern psychology attributes this effect to the work of the subconscious; Dante believes that the Grace of God has intervened. However one may interpret it, the experience itself is undeniable; and it is the Pilgrim's experience of such a mutation which is the matter of this canto.

In the bright morning sun, which is the same and not the same as other mornings filled with work ahead, the Pilgrim learns the literal facts of his nocturnal shift: Lucia (Illuminating Grace) has carried him to this new point while he slept. Virgil, who sees by Reason, has followed; and now the Pilgrim in his turn catches up: he gets a factual and rationalized account of his mysterious translation. And though "Lucia," the crucial fact, means hardly more to him than she does to the uninstructed modern reader, at least the Pilgrim has what he needs to tackle the path immediately before him.

The rest of the canto (line 73 to the end) describes the scene before the gates of Purgatory. They are inside a narrow and inconspicuous fissure in the rocky cliff, approached by three steps, respectively white, "darker than perse," and blood red. The steps are guarded by an angel with a shining sword, who accepts the travellers when Virgil explains that it is Lucia who has brought them here. The Pilgrim, obeying Virgil, throws himself to the ground, strikes himself three times on his breast, and craves the mercy of entrance; upon which the Angel Guardian marks seven P's on his forehead with his sword, and opens the gates with two keys, a silver and a gold.

This scene, like the dream, is evidently packed with unspoken meanings, some of which have been elucidated by the commentators, while others are still disputed. I refer once more to the notes in the Temple Classics edition, which give all that most readers need, and provide at least an introduction to the problems of a learned exegesis. In general it is clear that both the visible properties (sword, keys, steps, and the like) and the ritual gesture of the Guardian and the Pilgrim, are signs of that same transition to Purgation which the dream in one way, and Virgil's account of Lucia's carrying of the Pilgrim in another way, have already presented. The whole scene before the gates is like an epiphany at the end of a Greek tragedy: a tableau, or visible setpiece at the end of a completed action, showing forth its meaning in terms of its visible results.

It is the style of this passage, rather than its ultimate interpretation, that I wish to consider, for the style imitates the Pilgrim's alert but myopic mental life in the new realm, and gives the reader his clue to sympathetic understanding. The first part of the canto—night, dawn, and the dream—feels "poetic" in our sense of the word; but the scene before the gates in the bright morning light lacks the imaginative fusion, and the resonance, of the more lyric opening sections. It seems to employ an arbitrary sign-language, the kind of bald allegorizing that Croce objects to. A reader of English will probably be reminded of Bunyan's wooden personifications, which add nothing to the moral concepts they stand for. This impression, of course, is wrong, for Dante's symbols refer, not to abstract concepts, but to other objective realities, and hence there is no single key to their elucidation; one discovers that as soon as one tries, with the help of the commentators, to make a complete interpretation of this passage. But the *effect* of a sign-language which, like traffic-signals, may be blankly obeyed without full understanding or assent, is certainly intended here. Dante warns us that the style of this passage is different: speaking as author, he introduces it as follows (line 70):

> Lettor, tu vedi ben com'io innalzo
> la mia materia, e però con più arte
> non ti maravigliar s'io la rincalzo.

> (Reader, you clearly see how I make higher
> my subject-matter; if then with greater art
> I now sustain it, that is not surprising.)

Coleridge's famous distinction between the poetry of Imagination and the poetry of Fancy throws a good deal of light on the change of style, or "art," between the first part of the canto and the second. "In Imagination," Coleridge writes, "the parts of the meaning—both as regards the ways in which they are apprehended and the modes of combination of their effects in the mind—mutually modify one another." That is exactly what occurs in the poetry of night, dawn, and dream. "In Fancy," on the other hand, says Coleridge, "the parts of the meaning are apprehended as though independent of their fellow members . . . and although, of course, the parts together have a joint effect which is not what it would be if the assemblage were different, the effects of the parts remain for an interval separate, and combine or collide *later*, in so far as they do so at all." That describes very accurately the effect of the brilliant scene before the gates: each element is clear and separate, sharply actual; but they are not combined in a satisfying imaginative fusion. Because keys, sword, steps, and the rest *are* separate—a collection rather than a compound—they seem to demand some further effort on the part of reader and Pilgrim to make them combine "later."

The shift in style or art is thus away from "Poetry" as Coleridge, Croce, and many other proponents of the modern *mystique* have taught us to understand Poetry, and into a more positivistic mode of composition. For Coleridge, Fancy was an inferior style, based not upon the mode of awareness which is the source of Poetry as such, but upon the work of the discursive reason. What then does Dante mean by telling us that the daylight passage shows "greater art"? Does he mean to reject Poetry and its insights as inferior to what the waking mind can show when it is in contact with the discrete facts of its actual situation?

It is probable that Dante was proud of the rational ingenuity (or "art" in the sense of artifact) with which he devised the scene before the gates, fitting it into his whole elaborate symbolic structure. Moreover this scene is literally "higher" than the *Antipurgatorio*; it is not only the end of the night, but the basis of a new movement, an unfamiliar setting still to be explored. By breaking the texture of his narrative and speaking out as author, Dante breaks our identification with the Pilgrim, and bids us consider the development of the poem as poem. He may therefore wish us to admire not only the art of this particular passage, but the *change* of art and, in general, the extraordinary flexibility of the art of the whole canto, in which the perspectives of poetry, mythopoeia, dream, and wakeful rationality are imitated successively, each in its appropriate "art" or mode of composition.

From this more detached point of view we may divine the subject-matter of the canto as a whole: it is the Pilgrim's crucial change of heart. He tries to understand this change in various ways; but it is essentially something which happens *to* him, beyond his will and understanding, and for this reason all his ways of understanding are inadequate, and it is beyond his strength to pull them together. On the other hand, none of them is simply wrong: what Virgil tells him in the morning, what he sees at the gates, are simply other ways of understanding what he vaguely and suggestively grasped in dream. The whole sequence presents that rhythmic alternation of poetic contemplation and rational-moral effort which will be repeated in many varied figures, in many different regions, on the way up the Mountain.

But Canto ix has its own unity; it "imitates" one action of the Pilgrim, which ends. This action—his fluctuating and sharply-varied effort to grasp what is happening to him—is clearly suggested in the figure with which the canto ends. The gates open, and the Pilgrim hears singing within:

> Tale imagine appunto mi rendea
> ciò ch'io udiva, qual prender si suole
> quando a cantar con organi si stea:
> che or sì or no s'intendon le parole.

(Just such an image-in-the-mind was offered
  by that which I was hearing, as we are wont
   to get from people singing with an organ:
when now the words are clear, and now are not.)

𝕫𝕨 CHAPTER 5. ON THE DRAMATIC
COHERENCE OF THE CANTO

IN THE LAST CHAPTER I endeavored to show the poetic-dramatic coherence of Canto IX, in which the Pilgrim goes to sleep in the *Antipurgatorio*, dreams, and wakes in the morning before the gates of Purgatory proper. That canto reflects, I believe, one action (or *moto spiritale*, "movement of spirit," as Virgil will call it in Canto XVIII, line 32)—the Pilgrim's effort to understand his mysterious translation to the new realm. This action is prepared as the Pilgrim sinks to sleep, reaches its center or climax in his dream, and ends as the gates open.

These studies are all based upon this type of "dramatic" analysis of the *Purgatorio*, canto by canto. I now wish to offer a few general observations upon the purposes and methods of this approach to the poem.

It is evident that in Canto IX the imagery alone does not lead very directly to the coherence of the whole unit. The sensuous imagery is different at each stage of the developing action, as the Pilgrim grasps his experience now in one way, and now in another. Even the "art" of writing varies sharply, as Dante himself asks us to notice. The traditional symbolism of the canto—the ultimate meanings of the Eagle, Lucia, the three steps, the sword, and the rest—also does not *alone* show us what this particular canto is about. One might, with the aid of the commentators, construct a fairly consistent philosophical-theological interpretation of this canto, and its place in Dante's blueprints for his poem, by considering the meanings of those traditional symbols. But that would be to disregard the poem which Dante actually wrote; and it would, I think, do some violence to his own plan of composition, which is also a plan for the proper reading of the poem. According to this plan (as I have mentioned before) the "interpretation" is to be reached, not by looking up the answers at the back of the book, but by following "the development of the form." This developing form may be called *dramatic*, for it closely reflects, or imitates, the movements of the Pilgrim's growing and groping spirit. And each canto, for all the variety of its detail, presents the beginning, middle, and end of one such *moto spirital*.

Eliot remarks that a canto of the *Divine Comedy* corresponds to a whole play of Shakespeare's, and the *Divine Comedy* as a whole to all of Shakespeare's work. This observation is not meant to be applied literally, but it throws some light both upon Shakespeare's forms and upon Dante's. Thus, we have recently learned to see that in a play of Shakespeare's the sensuous imagery, the characters, the situation and the plot, and the "thought," are all organic parts of the composition, and cannot therefore be properly understood separately. This is also true of a canto of the *Divine Comedy*. For example, there are passages in the *Divine Comedy* in which a "thought" is presented (by Virgil or Marco Lombardo, or in an interpolation by the author) with the conceptual clarity and the logical connections which we associate with philosophy rather than poetry. One is tempted to accept such clear statements as giving the author's ultimate and full meaning—as though, after so much poetizing, he had decided suddenly to break down and tell all. But all of the philosophizing in the *Divine Comedy* is the utterance of a particular character in a particular situation. And for that reason it would be as bad a mistake to suppose that it gives the author's full meaning, as it would be to take an utterance by Othello or Gloucester as an utterance by Shakespeare. In both cases, what the characters say shows something about them, and one aspect of the situation they are describing; but it is only a part of the meaning of the poem in which it occurs. The context is all-important—in Shakespeare, the play as a whole; in Dante, the canto as a whole.

The *Divine Comedy* is so beautifully composed that, ideally, the whole poem should be the context in which any passage is read. It is woven of many recurrent themes; at any point what has gone before and what is yet to come are implicit; and the forward movement never ceases completely until the end. The cantos form parts of larger units (like the Days on the Mount of Purgatory); they are like waves on top of a larger ground-swell. But it would be impossible to hold all of this in mind at once. It would have been impossible for Dante himself to grasp it all simultaneously, in full awareness of each vital aspect—and even more impossible for him to write it that way. He did not try to do so. He made it in units appropriate to the natural limitations both of the poet and the reader. With the beginning of each canto he takes, as it were, a new breath, for a new act of poem-making, which will closely reflect a new movement of the Pilgrim's psyche. He expects the reader, also, to take a new breath, in order to grasp the new development of the whole poem which the canto will present; and then, perhaps, to pause long enough to explore its complex and significant coherence. This coherence—the poetic-dramatic form of the canto—is the context in which the ideas, the narratives, the characters, the judgments, and the lyric passages are to be understood.

In order to grasp a canto in this way the reader must make a new effort of perception. Even between cantos which are very closely connected in matter and manner, there is a slight but crucial shift of focus, demanding the very alert attention of the reader. And if one thinks of several cantos from different parts of the poem, it is evident that they are composed, if not on different principles, at least with emphases so different as to make them in effect different kinds of poetic units.

Canto IX, for example, is difficult to grasp as a whole on first reading because its actual texture is so varied. What goes on in that canto is far below the surface—a change in the Pilgrim which he does not himself fully grasp, yet so fundamental that it adumbrates the whole purgatorial process. On the other hand, the unity of Canto XV, and the unity of Canto

XVI, are evident at once because each is dominated by very consistent sensuous imagery, in Canto XV that of glaring light, in Canto XVI that of close darkness. Some cantos are dominated by a personality so strong, touching, and unique that the reader is impressed by it immediately. Canto V of the *Inferno*, for example, is Francesca's canto; for her being and destiny, as we get it in her own words, is by far the sharpest instance of the mode of being which the canto as a whole presents. Piccarda de Donati dominates her canto (*Paradiso* III) in a closely analogous way—it is even probable, I think, that Dante meant us to feel the analogy between a simple loving woman on the threshold of Hell, and a simple loving woman on the threshold of Heaven. But I do not mean to suggest, by these examples, that a canto is ever to be understood by means of its imagery or its characters alone. The emphasis on glaring light or close darkness in Cantos XV and XVI conveys a certain sharply-limited focus of the inner life, but that is presented in many other ways also in those cantos, as I shall try to show below. The emphasis on Francesca and Piccarda, in their cantos, tells us a great deal about the "new direction which love takes" at those moments; but for all the beauty of those women, it would be a bad mistake to neglect their context, the cantos in which each of them is one element only.

A single canto of the *Divine Comedy* is not·the whole poem, but it is far more than a mere slice of about 140 lines. It is an *organic part* of the whole poem. It is, therefore, the smallest unit in which Dante's principles of composition may be adequately studied. And it is the smallest context we are justified in considering, if we are to understand the characters, the narratives, the lyric passages, and the philosophizing, as Dante wished them to be understood.

PART TWO

THE ANCIENT PATH TO SELF-KNOWLEDGE
(THE SECOND DAY: CANTOS X-XVIII)

✿ CHAPTER 6. VIRGIL'S GUIDANCE

"ALL things that surround us, and all things that happen to us," said Coleridge, "have but one common final cause, namely the increase of consciousness in such wise that whatever part of the terra incognita of our nature the increased consciousness discovers, our will may conquer and bring into subjection to itself under the sovereignty of reason." This is Coleridge's romantic and Kantian faith, his description of the life of the growing soul as it ideally would be. It applies in a general way to the whole journey of the *Purgatorio*. But Dante was not romantic, or only romantic; his aspiration was corrected at every point by a sharp sense of actuality, his desire for what should be by his knowledge of what is. Thus Coleridge's words apply only with qualifications to the *Antipurgatorio*, for there the Pilgrim, looking about him with the eye of childhood, sees nothing which would enlighten the moral will with reason. But as soon as he is within the gates of Purgatory proper his experience begins to approach Coleridge's ideal. All things that surround him and happen to him serve to make him more aware of his own nature, the fallible life of the human spirit. The blank terrace of Pride, the smoke of Anger, show forth those states of the psyche; and as the soul becomes aware of itself its will is made free to respond to what Reason reveals of its true nature and destiny.

Dante believed that this path toward self-knowledge was as old as the culture of antiquity, and he built the ancient wisdom into the very structure of the Mountain path, the route which the soul in its quest for freedom and understanding *must* take. Virgil is the guide on this path, and by the end, in the evening of the second Day, in Canto XVIII, he has taught the Pilgrim to understand the infinitely various journeys of the human spirit, moved by love, in the light of his own pagan wisdom.

It is true that Virgil has conducted the Pilgrim all the way from the Dark Wood itself. In Hell, and even in the homesick foothills of the *Antipurgatorio*, he led him by the hand, supplying strength and encouragement, and giving only such literal explanations of the geography of the journey as the Pilgrim needed to negotiate the immediate road before him. But once within the gates he can begin to show the Pilgrim the principles of his own guidance; he can begin to make his charge a master and a seer in his own right.

We know from the plan of the *Divine Comedy* as a whole approximately what role Dante assigned to Virgil in the drama of spiritual growth. Virgil is not responsible for the very beginning of the journey, for he was sent by Beatrice to rescue Dante when he had lost his way. He will not conduct Dante to the end, for when Beatrice appears in the *Paradiso Terrestre*, Virgil is gone. But he is the means of the Pilgrim's escape from Hell, and of his attainment of man's earthly end; he can show him all that human reason, the *lumen naturale*, "natural light," as the Middle Ages called it, can reveal of human nature and destiny. He represents the whole culture of antiquity which Dante's time was rediscovering.

What the revival of classical culture meant in Dante's Europe, and in the *Commedia* which is the epic of that rebirth, is only now beginning to be clear to us. The reader who wishes to get some conception of the historic importance of this movement should consult Professor Curtius's great study of the Latin Middle Ages, the seed of Europe. The confidence that a natural order in the life of the individual and in society had been discovered and could be found again, came with the classics, and with the sense of their meaning for actual human life. For Dante, and for his time in general, Virgil's *Aeneid*, which celebrates the moral and political order of Rome, was the sign and the way of the old humane vision, "the weather-beaten Roman road from the ancient to the modern world," as Professor Curtius puts it.

For Dante, Virgil had also a more intimate value: he

guided him to the mastery of the art of poetry which he had to have in writing the *Commedia*; and that is acknowledged again and again in the poem itself. "As an opening chord," Professor Curtius writes, "Dante used his meeting with the ancient poets and his admission into their circle." The reference is to the Castle of Pagan sages in Limbo (*Inferno*, Canto IV) to which Virgil leads the Pilgrim at the beginning of the journey. "It is they who must legitimize his poetic mission," Professor Curtius continues. They are "united in an ideal society: a 'school of beauty,' (*la bella scuola*) of timeless authority." So Dante figures in his poem what Virgil did for him in life, as the reading of the *Aeneid* opened up his individual path as poet, his own "mission" of revealing everyman's path. The Pilgrim does not understand all this in the *Inferno*; he begins to understand it here in the second Day in Purgatory, as the nature of his own growth and the timeless truth of Virgil's guidance slowly become clear to him together.

Of course Dante the author, with his tough realism, knew that there must always be something a bit ghostly about the wisdom of the past, however abstractly true it may be, however timeless its authority. He knew, with hellish intensity, that his Florence was not the ideal city as Virgil, in Rome, suggested it. He knew that the Virgil whose presence is felt in the *Commedia* as a father, a guide, a gentle spirit, was not flesh and blood. We shall see that as the Pilgrim comes to the end of this Day, and learns what Virgil can teach him, he approaches the knowledge which Dante the author had all along: Virgil cannot finally satisfy him; his wisdom is not enough.

Dante also knew, as he planned the journey of the second Day, that it must stand for a process of development which, in life, takes years. If the *Antipurgatorio* is like childhood, the second Day is like adolescence, the attainment of manhood, when the individual is supposed to have enough moral strength and enough understanding to take a responsible place in his society. That is why the rhythm of the Day's journey is so slow in the beginning, and why Virgil, hovering over his charge, can explain things to him only bit by bit, as the occasion offers, and as the Pilgrim himself needs to know. Virgil is, in effect, leading him from childhood to maturity, where he can at last initiate him into the freedom of his timeless society, the classical human city.

∂● CHAPTER 7. THE PATTERN OF LIBERATION

THE JOURNEY of the second Day is in two main parts, Cantos X-XIV, in which the Pilgrim toils upward slowly, by muscular and moral effort, understanding little; and Cantos XV-XVIII, when he ascends more easily as his understanding and freedom increase together. In this chapter I wish to consider a few features of the first half of the Day, Cantos X-XIV. The Pilgrim himself hardly knows what he is doing here, but he gains the experience which he needs for the intellectual effort with which the Day ends, Cantos XV-XVIII.

Dante has built into the path up the Mountain the rhythmic sequence of spiritual growth, as I observed in the last chapter. So that if one thinks over the literal narrative of the Pilgrim's climb, which traces the ancient path from terrace to terrace, one may see clearly how Dante understood the plot, or abstract pattern, of the soul's struggle for freedom.

Thus in Canto X the Pilgrim and Virgil climb up the difficult trail to the first ledge, and look about them. The first impression is that of an empty, rocky desolation; then the Pilgrim sees, cut into the rock of the Mountain wall, a frieze of humble figures: the Virgin Mary, David, and Trajan. Next he makes out the repentant proud, so bowed under their burdens of stone that he does not at first realize that they are human. He hears their stories, and learns about their present plight. As he leaves this terrace he sees, cut into the stone beneath his feet, thirteen images of the fallen proud, from Satan to Troy. Then the angel of the stair invites the travellers to ascend, and they climb to the next terrace, where Envy is purged (Canto XII, line 76 ff.). In Canto XIII we enter the terrace of Envy, and there again the first impression is that of empty rock. Then we hear three voices, the Virgin Mary's, Orestes', and one repeating Christ's admonition, "Love them from whom ye have suffered evil." And then, as in the preceding terrace, the repentant spirits appear: the envious with their eyes wired shut, and we hear their stories. Leaving this terrace and its denizens, we hear the voices of Cain and of Aglauros (Canto xiv, line 130 ff.) whom Envy ruined.

It is clear that the path through Pride and the path through Envy are analogous: the parts of the two little journeys correspond, though literally they are quite different. First we are reminded, visibly or audibly, of virtuous spirits from legend or history. Then we meet those who are resuffering the evil motivations which moved them on earth; but now the evil is perceived (in the light of the possibility of virtue) not as it appeared on earth, but as it actually affects the psyche, weighing it down to the ground or blinding it. The stories of these spirits bring the experience home to the Pilgrim, for they speak of the Italy he knows. Continuing on the upward path, the evil we have just been through is made visible or audible in legendary or historic figures; and then we are free to move on. Thus the scene itself—the literally-perceptible path as the Pilgrim follows its changing course—indicates the plot of the drama of purgation. We are to understand that the spirits we meet are living through this drama with unimaginable slowness, though when we see them they are caught (for years) in the resuffering of their evil passions, and are not yet free to move on. The Pilgrim in his upward progress also goes through this dramatic sequence. But what I wish to consider here is neither the action-and-passion of the repentant spirits, nor that of the Pilgrim, but the abstract *form* of purgation as the path in its successive sights and sounds reveals it.

Virgil gives the Pilgrim a hint about the nature of this path as soon as he thinks it will be understood: in Canto xiii. The Pilgrim has traversed the blank rock of Pride with some of the grimness he acquired in Hell. But as he left that terrace, responding to the angel's invitation to ascend, he felt for the first time the difference between the issueless passions of the lost and the passion of purgation; and he asks

Virgil what the voices he hears (those of the love of neighbor) may be. Virgil answers (line 37):

E'l buon maestro: "Questo cinghio sferza
la colpa dell'invidia, e però sono
tratte da amor le corde della ferza.
Lo fren vuol esser del contrario suono;
credo che l'udirai, per mio avviso,
prima che giunghi al passo del perdono."

(And the good master said: "This circle scourges
the sin of envy, and from love are drawn,
therefore, the thongs with which to make the scourges.
The bit must needs be of contrary sound;
I think, by what I've learned, that you will hear it
before the pass where pardon will be found.")

Virgil refers directly to the terrace of envy which they are entering, but his formula applies to the repeated rhythm of liberation which is embodied in the path. Love, like a whip, drives the human spirit to resuffer its evil or mistaken impulses which have hardened into habit. It is always love which drives us; in Purgatory it is love for the unseen "better," as the first line said. But this love appears in countless forms, as humility, for instance, in the first terrace. The "bit" pulls against the whip of love: it is the evil motive, not as it appeared on earth in its illusory attractiveness, but as it appears here *sub specie aeternitatis*, in the color of rock, the sights and sounds of human suffering. It can be clearly seen (or "heàrd" as Virgil says here, thinking of Cain's voice, and Aglauros's) only when it has been gone through again as it *is*. But when the spirit thus perceives its evil motive, it is free to take a different direction. The passions of Hell are suffered to no further end; those of purgatory as impediments to be traversed in the upward path of the spirit driven by its freedom-seeking love.

One may appreciate the psychological accuracy of Virgil's

formula by considering some little repentance of one's own—"repenting" a stupid mistake made in public, for instance. One is driven by offended self-love to rehearse the painful scene in memory: to relive the fatuous impulse, not as it looked when it was obeyed, but as it looks in a later and truer perspective. Only after suffering and seeing enough is one free to dismiss the matter and turn to pleasanter thoughts. Psychoanalysis is supposed to assist this process: to free the human from his compulsions by leading him to relive and so understand them.

"The branch of philosophy which regulates the work in its whole and in its parts," Dante wrote to Can Grande, about his *Commedia*, "is morals or ethics, because the whole was undertaken not for speculation but for practical results." This the Pilgrim begins to understand as soon as he is inside the gates of purgatory; he begins to get the practical results himself: to move out of his state of misery and on toward felicity, as Dante puts it in the same *Letter*. It is this movement-of-spirit, through suffering to freedom and understanding—ethics not as a static scheme but as a *way*—which governs the whole poem and its parts. That is why these central cantos of the *Purgatorio* throw light on the whole journey, that of Hell which is behind us, and that of Heaven which is still far ahead. These cantos are the best place also in which to study Dante's didactic purpose in writing the *Commedia*—something much deeper and more ambitious than education as we know it.

The classical conception of the learning process may be put (as Mr. Burke has explained) in the formula, *poiema, pathema, mathema*; making (or doing), suffering, knowledge. Plato and Aristotle both thought that man had to learn by *doing* first: trying something and suffering the consequences; only then could he come to know consciously and intellectually. Both of them prescribed practical training for the young as a preliminary to intellectual training: gymnastics, music, the inculcation of the right habits through experience, and *then* the philosophy which frees the learner, makes him his own master. They described in their rational terms a process like that Saint Paul had in mind when he said that the Law was a schoolmaster to bring the Hebrews to the new freedom and understanding represented by Christ's commandment, the principle behind the Law. These insights were at the basis of traditional education in the western world for at least six hundred years—the phrase liberal (or *freeing*) arts echoes it faintly even to our time. The Progressive educators (who pay more attention to the *process* of learning than anyone else) confirm the ancient insights when they tell us that the student learns first "by doing."

Dante built this ancient and not quite lost lore of learning into the basic plan of the poem, that of a *developing* form; he built it with special clarity into the changing path up the Mountain. But in doing so he was not thinking of education as something to be had apart from the struggle of life itself. He thought that the human spirit, when moving in the right direction, lived in this rhythm. That is why he is not didactic in the manner of other authors who set out to teach and preach. His didactic purpose coincides with his purpose as artist; propaganda is swallowed up in contemplation. I have pointed out in another place that the formula *poiema, pathema, mathema* describes the form of Sophoclean tragedy, which imitates the beginning, middle, and end of a complete action, or *moto spiritale*. The rhythm of the *Purgatorio* is tragic in that sense; in many analogous figures, wisdom is acquired through effort and suffering. The reader, in his turn, is to be freed and enlightened through pity, which joins him to the human sufferer, and terror, which joins him to the secret cause.

In the course of the four cantos we are considering, Dante the Pilgrim traverses two terraces, that of Pride and that of Envy, and so sees the form of the path twice. But though the abstract form is the same, the actual paths in the two terraces are different; and in this difference we may see the pattern of purgation in another way. In the terrace of Pride, for instance, the humble at the beginning and the proud at the end are unspeaking sculptures. The effect of walking over the thirteen intaglios of the fall of pride is like that of a heavy beating; one is reminded of Virgil's description (*Inferno*, Canto VII) of those who trust worldly power abased by Fortuna's turning wheel—or of *De Casibus* and the *Mirror for Magistrates*. It is the theme of the collision between human presumption and the nature of things, a moral *lieu commun* for generations. But in Dante's scheme this vision is the merest beginning of wisdom. In the next terrace the life of love reaches us with the intimacy of the voice and the intelligibility of words. The repentant envious (in contrast to the proud) look extremely human from the first: their upturned faces, defenceless, their eyes wired shut, show the true blindness of envy, which, on earth, is disguised by envy's proneness to malicious peeking. And the voices of Cain and Aglauros, coming and going like thunder in mountain country, start many echoes in our minds, and prepare the movement of the second part of the Day's journey. Thus the shape of the path embodies the pattern of liberation, not only in each terrace, but in its whole course up the Mountain. Every time the pattern is repeated, human nature and destiny are more deeply and clearly revealed.

The form of the path, terrace by terrace, and from the gates of Purgatory to the evening of the second Day, thus *suggests* the form of the Pilgrim's inner life. But the successive actions whereby he ascends do not coincide with his literal, spatial movement through the successive terraces. The relation between his movement-of-spirit and the scenes of the climb (the "action-scene ratio," as Mr. Kenneth Burke calls it) varies continually. Sometimes his spirit takes a different direction in the middle of a terrace. Canto XI, for example, begins in the middle of the terrace of pride; and it is the canto, not the terrace, which shows the rhythmic unit of the Pilgrim's own spiritual progress as he explores the path which so many have taken before him. If one were to follow the Pilgrim's growth in detail, it would be necessary to investigate the developing form of each canto. That I do not attempt here. Instead I shall offer two samples of his progress, one from Canto x, the beginning of the sequence, the other from Canto xiv, near the end. The difference between his movement-of-spirit in the beginning, and his movement-of-spirit at the end shows his growth in freedom and understanding, during the first half of the Day.

As soon as the gates of Purgatory have closed behind Virgil and his charge, they must start (without looking back) a steep climb to the first terrace on the flank of the Mountain (Canto x, line 7):

> Noi salivam per une pietra fessa,
>   che si moveva d'una e d'altra parte,
>   sì come l'onda che fugge e s'appressa.
> "Qui si convien usare un poco d'arte,"
>   cominciò il duca mio, "in accostarsi,
>   or quinci or quindi, al lato che si parte."
> E ciò fece li nostri passi scarsi
>   tanto, che pria lo scemo della luna
>   rigiunse al letto suo per ricorcarsi,
> che noi fossimo fuor di quella cruna.

> (We were climbing upward through a cleft rock,
>   which was moving on this and on that side,
>   as sea-waves will approach and then depart.
> "Just here a little skill must be applied,"
>   began my leader, "always to bring your steps,
>   this way and that, to the receding side."
> And our paces became therefore so scarce
>   that before the moon, now growing feeble,
>   returned to bed to sink again to rest,
> we had come through the eye of that needle.)

This passage has its overtones of meaning; but its style (which imitates, as always, the Pilgrim's mode of awareness) is close and literal. It appeals to kinesthetic memory, and its effect is to give the sense of a muscular equilibrium, a physical feat. It is a figure of the beginning of the moral life as ancient wisdom prescribes it: obedience without understanding. Virgil is here more like a coach (of track, or singing, or acting) than he is like a lecturer. The passage between wavering walls reminds one of Aristotle's rule of thumb: to aim, in all the varied contingencies of the moral life, for a middle way between opposite dangers. The figure itself is like one of Aristotle's: the passage between Scylla and Charybdis by immediate, empirical skill. So the Pilgrim proceeds, slowly, to explore the terraces of Pride and Envy.

But as he goes the mind awakens; his own spirit proceeds from doing, through suffering, toward understanding. It was in the transition from the terrace of Pride to that of Envy that Virgil told him about the "whip of love" and the opposing "bit." And in Canto xiv his movement-of-spirit reaches a climax and turning-point.

In the drama of the second Day, Canto xiv corresponds to Cantos v and vi, which mark the climax and turning-point in the pathetic drama of the first Day in the *Antipurgatorio*. In the first Day the climax was expressed by the image of the down-rushing river, followed by Dante's great lament over Italy. Here in Canto xiv the down-rushing river reappears: it is the Arno, and the Pilgrim introduces it by a very effective periphrasis (line 16): "Through the midst of Tuscany there spreads a stream." Guido del Duca picks up the Pilgrim's cue, and gives the downward course of the river, as though into Hell, past the deepening degradation of the Casentines, the Aretines, the Florentines, and the Pisans. And from that beautiful image he goes directly into a lament over the state of Romagna, which parallels Dante's own lament over Italy in Canto vi.

The drama of the first Day, however, is a Pathos; and the

Pilgrim's need to understand human folly and evil in its downward course is thwarted. The drama of the second Day is ethical, and its turning-point here in Canto XIV shows how his suffering, the result of moral effort, begins to yield light. Guido del Duca introduces his diatribe against Romagna with a fundamental question, which is not merely rhetorical; it expresses among other things the new, more rational direction which the Pilgrim's quest is taking (line 86):

> O gente umana, perchè poni il core
> là 'v'è mestier di consorto divieto?

> (O race of humans, why do you fix your heart
> where partnership needs must be excluded?)

As the travellers come to the end of Envy, and sense its true nature in the voices of Cain and of Aglauros (a crash of thunder repeated quickly and fading quickly), Virgil assists the Pilgrim's new need for understanding as follows (line 142):

> Già era l'aura d'ogni parte queta,
>   ed ei mi disse: "Quel fu il duro camo,
>   che dovria l'uom tener dentro a sua meta.
> Ma voi prendete l'esca sì che l'amo
>   dell'antico avversario a sè vi tira;
>   e però poco val freno o richiamo.
> Chiamavi il cielo, e intorno vi si gira,
>   mostrandovi le sue bellezze eterne,
>   e l'occhio vostro pure a terra mira;
> onde vi batte chi tutto discerne."

> (The air again was quiet all around,
>   and he said to me: "That was the hard bit
>   which ought to hold man in his proper bound.
> But you so seize the bait with the hook in it
>   that the old enemy to himself can draw you;
>   little avails then either call or bit.

The heavens meanwhile in their circling call you,
displaying to you their eternal beauty,
and your eye fixed on the earth before you;
therefore he beats you who perceives all clearly.")

This passage, with its mixed metaphors and its laconic allusions to what is past and to what is to come, is so tightly-
packed that the reader (like the Pilgrim) can hardly be
expected to sort out its implications immediately. The "bit"
in this passage refers to Virgil's previous explanation which
I quoted above. Here it takes the form of the voices, and they
(through the association with thunder, the traditional voice
of God) become God's own restraining force. The "call" of
heaven, presented as the visible beauty of the stars, corresponds to the "whip of love" in Virgil's first formula, the
aspiration for the better which moves the soul toward light
and freedom. The last line pulls everything together: both
the hope and the torment of the Pilgrim's progress are due
to the *truth* of human nature and destiny, the all-seeing eye
of God. So the immediate struggle is revealed in the wider
setting of the whole Mountain, and of the stars which circle
above it in their alluring light and order. But the tight style
of the passage shows that, in the Pilgrim's awareness, the
wider perspective is too much, his understanding still inchoate.

The form of the drama of liberation is embodied in the
path up the Mountain. It is also realized in the rhythm of
the Pilgrim's inner life, which always moves from the letter
to the spirit, from what the physical eye shows to the meaning for human life. In the next chapters I shall return to the
Pilgrim, as he explores the insights which dawn upon him
in Canto xiv, the turning point of the second Day's journey,
when moral effort gives place to the struggle of the mind.

🐝 CHAPTER 8. CANTO XV: THE LIGHT OF THE MIND

IN THE LITERAL STORY of the climb up the Mountain, Canto xv recounts the ascent which Virgil and the Pilgrim make from the terrace of Envy to the terrace of Anger. It thus corresponds to the climb from Pride to Envy: it is a transition from one mode of the spirit's life to another. Whenever the Pilgrim climbs from one terrace to another, he changes, and he thinks over the general nature of the journey. But this transition is almost as fundamental as that accomplished during the first night, from the *Antipurgatorio* to the beginning of purgation. It marks a reorientation of the Pilgrim's inner being, a turn from the obedient moral effort of Cantos x-xiv, to the effort to *understand* his own being and its destiny.

In the last chapter I pointed out that some sort of insight, half-understood, was dawning in the Pilgrim. In Canto xv Dante presents it in the metaphor of light. The whole Canto is full of light of many kinds. We cannot assign any single meaning to this light. I suppose Dante was thinking of an experience which everyone has to some degree at some time, the feeling that understanding is possible, that important knowledge lies just ahead. The Pilgrim tries, with Virgil's aid, to reduce this inchoate illumination to reason; but it turns out to be too much for him. Canto xv is only the beginning of the action which does not end until night falls in Canto xviii, at the end of the Day. It is the prologue to the drama of the awakened mind, the struggle to understand the psyche's life in terms of its own natural reason.

The excess of light and the effort to deal with it are sharply presented in the opening sequence, as the travellers come around the flank of the Mountain and meet the late level beams of the sun (line 7):

E i raggi ne ferian per mezzo il naso,
    perchè per noi girato era sì il monte
    che già dritti andavamo in ver l'occaso,
quand'io senti' a me gravar la fronte
    allo splendore assai più che di prima,
    e stupor m'eran le cose non conte:
ond'io levai le mani in ver la cima
    delle mie ciglia, e fecimi il solecchio
    che del soperchio visibile lima.

(On the bridge of the nose the rays struck us now,
    for we had circled the Mountain, and our way
    was leading straight toward where the sun goes down,
when I felt upon my brow the sudden weight,
    far greater than before, of light shining,
    and things not understood held me amazed:
wherefore I lifted my hands upward, trying
    above my eyes to make me that sun-shade
    with which one files away excessive brightness.)

The glare of the sun is less brilliant than the angel of the stair. Both are associated with the mathematical clarity of the formula (lines 16-21), the angle of incidence is equal to the angle of reflection.

As soon as the Pilgrim has partially recovered, he tries to deal with one of the insights we saw him receive in the last canto, Guido's distinction between goods which can be shared and goods which cannot, which I quoted above. He asks Virgil what Guido could have meant, and Virgil replies as follows (line 49):

"Perchè s'appuntan li vostri disiri
    dove per compagnia parte si scema,
    invidia move il mantaco ai sospiri.
Ma se l'amor della spera suprema
    torcesse in suso il desiderio vostro,
    non vi sarebbe al petto quella tema:

chè per quanti si dici più lì 'nostro,'
   tanto possiede più di ben ciascuno,
    e più di caritate arde in quel chiostro."

("Because the focal point of your desires
   is where each sharer lessens each one's share,
    envy impels the bellows of your sighs.
But if that love which is of the highest sphere
   twisted upward the longings which are yours,
    you would not have within your heart such fear:
for the more there are there who say 'ours,'
   the more of good each one of them possesses,
    and the more charity in that cloister glows.")

The distinction between material goods which cannot be shared, and spiritual goods which can, is to be found in Plato, notably in the *Symposium*, where there is a hierarchy of loves, from the love of a particular object at the bottom of the scale, to a freed and sharable love like Diotima's, for "The Good" or "The Beautiful" at the top. Dante might have read about this in Boethius. It is also to be found in Aristotle, notably in his hierarchy of friendships in Books VIII and IX of the *Nicomachean Ethics*, or in his account of life in the service of the intellect, in Book x. As pagan sage and master of Natural Reason, Virgil can see and expound this fundamental point. We can even see it in our time, for it is obvious that the more there are who love a beefsteak, the less of it any of them can enjoy; while the more there are who love a symphony, the greater the enjoyment of each, as the delighted understanding of the work spreads from the composer, to the conductor, to the strings and woodwinds and other performers, and thence to the audience.

But though Virgil as master of Natural Reason has a right to this insight, he does not explain it to the Pilgrim in the moral, psychological, and esthetic analogies I used above. He talks about the "highest sphere," referring to Aristotelian

cosmology and theology, and to the "theatre" of the whole
Mount of Purgatory, with the stars above. In Dante's composition this visible scene of many stories is of course contained
within a Christian view; and Virgil knows that formally;
he knows that what he can explain about the light which
here touches the mind does not plumb the full meaning.

As for the Pilgrim, he cannot even follow what Virgil says.
He is still not used to the light of truth, still gets darkness
from true light because of his focus on the earthly or material, as Virgil tells him (lines 64-66); and continues:

> "Quello infinito ed ineffabil bene
>   che è lassù, così corre ad amore,
>   come a lucido corpo raggio viene.
> Tanto si dà, quanto trova d'ardore,
>   sì che quantunque carità si estende,
>   cresce sopr'essa l'eterno valore;
> e quanta gente più lassù s'intende,
>   più v'è da bene amare, e più vi s'ama,
>   e come specchio l'uno all'altro rende."

> ("That infinite and ineffable good
>   which is above us, ever runs to love,
>   as a ray of light to a bright body would.
> As much as it finds, it gives, of ardent love;
>   and so, as far as charity may extend,
>   increase comes, from the timeless power above;
> and the more folk, up there, who comprehend,
>   the more to love well, and the more love is there,
>   and each one mirrors back what others send.")

The imagery of reflected warmth and light is here very evidently akin to the vastly expanded symbolism of light
throughout the *Paradiso*. And Dante uses very resonant
rhymes here, as he does, for example, in Canto XII of the
Paradiso (line 1 ff.) to give us the pleasure of musical harmony, to reinforce the echoing meanings with echoing

sounds, and, with both, to deepen the effects of the visual imagery. Consider, for instance, in the first passage, the rhymes *vostro, nostro, chiostro*, and in the second, *amore, ardore, valore*. Dante certainly intended this moment, when light first breaks upon us, as an intimation of beatitude. Virgil, watching the Pilgrim's excited bewilderment, knows this; and knows also that it is not beatitude, for in the next tercet (lines 76-78) he refers his charge to Beatrice, in one of his few uses of her name.

The Pilgrim does not have time to say that Virgil's last words are enough, for the different light of his dream of gentleness bursts upon him. He sees the Virgin Mary, Pisistratus, and St. Stephen, in the very act of charity, images of the same premonition of beatitude which Virgil had explained. This is the final form which the illumination takes: a day-dream so vivid that it reminds one of the nocturnal dream of Canto IX. He wakes from it in a similar way, to the facts of his immediate situation, which the physical eye can record. But now he knows that such mythic or imagined visions contain *their* truth: *i miei non falsi errori*, he calls them (line 117): "my not false errors." Virgil confirms this, in his final speech (lines 127-138). He had seen his charge absorbed in the dream; but he looked not with the eye of the body, but with his ghostly insight, and he saw that the Pilgrim's dreams were divinely inspired, to lure him toward his far-off goal.

Thinking over the canto as a whole, it appears that the light which touched the Pilgrim's mind as he left Envy behind must have been a premonition of the goal of his whole journey. He suddenly sensed that his motivation was to be understood in the light of its End. Not that he gets the vision of God which the *Paradiso* approaches in a thousand ways; he gets reflections of the divine light only, and even the reflections are too bright. Virgil's explanations are in terms of the reflections: the cosmic order, light glowing from mind to mind.

When the Pilgrim comes to himself after his day-dream, his waking, rational mind is unsatisfied. He is ready for the next stage of the journey, when in the smoke of anger he will struggle with the classic difficulties of reason, turning from what enlightens the mind to the needs of the rational mind itself. The visions of charity, ending his moment of illumination, serve also, like the visions of humility and love of neighbor which he got farther down the Mountain, to place the next struggle in the context of a wider truth.

🕿 CHAPTER 9. CANTO XVI:
REASON IN DARKNESS

According to the literal story of the climb, the Pilgrim reaches the realm of the repentant angry when he is overwhelmed by his visions of gentleness, near the end of Canto xv. But the more important change occurs with the beginning of Canto xvi, when he and Virgil enter the thick smoke which suggests the condition of anger itself, as the repentant must resuffer it. As usual, the Pilgrim and his guide must in some sense share the state of the repenting spirits in order to get ahead with their own journey; and their progress through the smoke reveals the nature of the very slow purgation which is accomplished here, and also places this mode of the soul's life in the wider perspective of the whole journey.

Thus Canto xvi is an act in the Pilgrim's drama of psychic growth; it shows a new use of the mind. Canto xv, when he was free to move upward, was all a glare of light; Canto xvi, when he must struggle with an impediment in his way, is all close darkness. Dante here uses sensuous imagery to indicate that the life of the psyche is concentrated in *one* of its faculties. The principle governing this use of imagery is well put in one of his author's interpolations, Canto iv, line 1 ff.:

> Quando per dilettanze ovver per doglie,
>   che alcuna virtù nostra comprenda,
>   l'anima bene ad essa si raccoglie,
> par che a nulla potenza più intenda;
>   e questo è contra quello error, che crede
>   che un' anima sopr'altra in noi s'accenda.
> E però, quando s'ode cosa o vede
>   che tenga forte a sè l'anima volta,
>   vassene il tempo, e l'uom non se n'avvede:
> ch'altra potenza è quella che l'ascolta,

ed altra quella che ha l'anima intera;
questa è quasi legata, e quella è sciolta.

(Whenever, through enjoyment or through pain
   which some one of our faculties receives,
   on it alone the whole soul concentrates,
its other powers, it seems, it does not heed:
   and this is contrary to that view, which errs,
   that soul, lit on soul, in us may come to be.
And therefore, when some thing is seen or heard
   which strongly bends the soul to it, to fix it,
   the time goes by, not seen by us, or heard:
for it is one power in us which thus listens,
   another that which the whole soul possesses:
   the first is bound, the latter uncommitted.)

In Canto XVI, the black-dark smoke suggests the confinement, or binding, of the soul; while the touch and the words
of Virgil, and the voices singing the *Agnus Dei*, suggest the
potentialities which the soul still has for freedom and the use
of all its faculties.

The one faculty which the Pilgrim does use here is discursive reason, the *word* of the logical mind. He clings to
Virgil (who always has reason) and listens to his admoni-
tions until he hears Marco Lombardo, who in his turn presents him with a reasoned discourse which ultimately frees
him from the confining smoke. The action of the canto is
thus a struggle of the reason, without the aid of the other
faculties, for freedom: "reason in darkness."

The smoke, or darkness, is appropriate both for the re-
suffered passion of anger, and for this moment in the Pilgrim's progress. We saw how in Canto XV the Pilgrim received more illumination than he could use; now he is like
a sophomore who has read too much, and is stumped and
thwarted by the contradiction between the ideal potentialities
of the life of the mind and its dark and irritating actuality.

Aristotle remarked that anger is the passion which is closest to reason, and anyone who has been angry will remember the sense of congested rationality, as though one had all the right reasons *inside*, which goes with that condition. Dante and Marco Lombardo treat each other with respect, and share a kind of noble grief which transcends anger; yet even as their reasoning leads toward freedom ahead, we are continually reminded of the anger which confines them. There is the irritation of the smoke itself; the annoyance of trying to talk to one who is invisible; the ineptitude of the Pilgrim's questions, and Marco's brusqueness thereat.

In this act of the mind's drama, Marco Lombardo replaces Virgil as guide or *raisonneur*. I suppose Dante had many converging reasons for using Marco. He was a Venetian courtier noted for his honor, liberality, and learning. He must have struggled nobly with the irrational darkness of Italian politics, and lost his temper, as Dante himself did. After the brilliant metaphysical poetry of Canto xv, Marco reminds us sharply of the difference between the ideal potentialities of the soul for light and harmony and its actual savage and myopic divisions, as Dante knew them in his own time and place. On the other hand, the noble Marco can remind us that though anger is an evil, there are things in human life and society beyond the individual's control, at which it is necessary to be angry—and that passion was apparently very congenial to Dante anyway.

Marco announces himself, through the thick darkness, with an abrupt question (line 25) which shows that he has overheard the Pilgrim and Virgil:

"Or tu chi se', che il nostro fummo fendi,
   e di noi parli pur come se tue
   partissi ancor lo tempo per calendi?"

("Now who are you, who come cleaving our smoke
   and speaking of us just as though, for you,
   time were still measured as the calends go?")

He knows that the Pilgrim is not in his timeless world beyond the grave, but alive in the *first* life, and hence subject to time. The Pilgrim's mortality is associated with the body in his reply:

> Con quella fascia
> che la morte dissolve men vo suso

> (With those wrappings
> which death dissolves, I take my upward way)

But then the wrappings of the flesh are associated with his "enclosure" in God's grace (line 40):

> e, se Dio m'ha in sua grazia richiuso

> (and, if God has in his grace enwrapped me)

The effect of these modulations is to extend the meanings of the dark smoke (which is the scene of the drama) to earthly life, in time and the flesh; and yet to remind us of the grace which promises escape. Similarly, Marco identifies himself laconically (lines 46-48) and as though impatiently, as one who *alone* aimed at the good on the dark earth, and then adds as an afterthought, "I pray you, pray for me, when you shall be on high" (lines 50-51). Thus we are made to feel that Marco and the Pilgrim are offended not only by the smoke which blinds them here, but by the darkness of Italy which they both remember.

In this situation, and this setting of many meanings, the Pilgrim asks the question which provokes Marco's discourse: granted the light he saw before the smoke came, and granted the actual darkness here and on earth, who is to blame: man, here below, or the "heavens?" It is an either-or question, based not upon perception but upon the discursive reason's demand for univocal concepts and logical concatenation. The Pilgrim is caught in the paradox of moral freedom and responsibility, one of the classic traps of the reason: he wants man to be *either* free and responsible, *or* determined, like the physical world, by the movements of the stars. The question itself betrays the Pilgrim's lack of perception, as Marco says at once, with a sigh of impatience:

"Frate,
lo mondo è cieco, e tu vien ben da lui."

("Brother,
the world is blind, and surely you come from it.")

Marco then (lines 67-84) gives with great elegance the classic account of the relations between moral freedom, the appetite for the Good native to man, and the compulsions of the physical world. I do not attempt to paraphrase this discourse, but I commend it to the reader, together with the illuminating notes in the Temple Classics edition.

What I do wish to point out is the *nature* of Marco's reply. It is, I think, a piece of dialectic akin to Plato's: that is, he proceeds to solve the paradox, not by logic, not in its own terms, but by making distinctions and seeking a more exact account of the actual process of human choice, the pursuit of good and the avoidance of evil. The effect is to lead us from the univocal concepts which the Pilgrim somewhat arrogantly demands, to a new perception; from the discursive or scientific reason (*episteme*) to the *nous* of Aristotle, which Mr. Philip Wheelwright translates as "apperceptive intelligence."

When he has reached that point, Marco can offer (lines 83-94) his beautiful image of the simple soul, before the confusions of the world divide it, as a joyful but heedless child. I have already quoted the first tercet of this passage in connection with the *Antipurgatorio*, for I believe it throws some light on the Pilgrim's obedient but unregenerate state in that realm. In this context, it has some of the illuminating and nostalgic quality of memory. For where we are *now* the soul is not thus whole and innocent, but divided, between

> . . . the imperatives of "is and seems"
> and may and may not, desire and control

as Mr. T. S. Eliot puts it in his (rather Pascalian) *Animula.*

The memory of that innocence, that wholeness of soul which precedes the first sharp sense of good and evil, suggests, however faintly, the possibility of another innocence and wholeness beyond this darkness. Pointing ahead, it leads Marco to the next part of his discourse, which has to do with the splits, the double doubts, and the totalitarian or absolute demands which divide human society, much as we have just seen the individual soul trapped by its worship of the one faculty of discursive reason, and so divided.

The simple soul, before the world and its own reason divide it, responds wholly to any good thing, however trifling or even illusory, which means that, without guidance, it may lose its way (line 94):

> Onde convenne legge per fren porre;
> convenne rege aver, che discernesse
> della vera cittade almen la torre.

> (Wherefore laws must be placed as reins to keep it;
> rulers there must be, able to discern
> the towers, at least, of the true city.)

The rulers of the human race, according to Marco, have the power and obligation to lead the souls in their charge. They are responsible for education in the widest and deepest sense. In this Marco agrees with Plato and Aristotle, both of whom founded their politics upon the appropriate sensuous, emotional, moral, and intellectual *training*, to be administered by the rulers of society and of the state. This view of the relations between ethics, education, and the state, with its corollary that the rulers are responsible for the "good life," survived into the late Renaissance, as one may clearly see by comparing James I's *Basilicon Doron* with Shakespeare's *Measure for Measure.*

But in fact our rulers do *not* see the towers of the true city, and lead us toward them; and their evil rule, says Marco (lines 103-104), is the reason for the world's actual badness, and not the corruption of human nature. Marco proceeds to describe the failure of the rulers, both ecclesiastical and political, by means of a traditional figure and several very sharp metaphors.

The first of these (a traditional figure) refers to the Thomistic interpretation of Leviticus 11.4: "Nevertheless these shall ye not eat of them that chew the cud, or of them that divide the hoof" (line 98):

il pastor che precede
ruminar può, ma non ha l'unghie fesse

(the shepherd who goes before
may chew the cud, but has not divided hooves)

Chewing the cud is supposed to mean understanding Scripture, having the hoof divided, the power to distinguish between various directions of the spirit. Marco means that the ecclesiastical authorities, though they may understand the Bible, cannot make the necessary distinctions, especially that between secular authority, based on Natural Reason, and ecclesiastical authority, based on traditional interpretation of Scripture. His use of the arbitrary sign-language of scriptural interpretation at this point probably reflects his impatience both with the Pilgrim and with the ecclesiastics he is thinking about. But he immediately proceeds to clarify his meaning in two powerful metaphors. The "sun"—natural reason—which ought to light the way of the world, and the "sun" of religion which ought to light the way to God, have put each other out (lines 106-109); and the sword of temporal rule has been joined to the crook of spiritual rule; the monstrous combination must perforce go badly. He then gives a passionate description of the condition of Lombardy, so dark and divided that only the wicked are safe there, except for one good old man. And then (line 127):

> "Di' oggimai che la Chiesa di Roma,
>   per confondere in sè due reggimenti,
>   cade nel fango, e sè brutta e la soma."

("Declare henceforward that the Church of Rome,
     by mixing in herself two powers of rule,
     falls in the filth, is stained, and stains her load.")

To understand Dante's own matured view of the relations between Church and State it is necessary to study his *De Monarchia*. What Marco says here does not literally contradict the doctrine of *De Monarchia*, with its anti-totalitarian insistence upon the authority, in its own realm, of Natural Reason, and its insistence upon the practical and theoretical necessity for separating Church and State. But Marco's remarks are brief, partial, and somewhat enigmatic. He himself is still resuffering his own dark anger, the result of his experience on earth; and he is addressing the Pilgrim who, at this moment, cannot cope with the whole problem, but only with that part of it which concerns the role of Natural Reason. I pointed out that the theme of secular and religious authority and guidance was adumbrated in the prophetic dream of Canto IX; it is resumed here in the context of the mind's drama. It will be approached historically during the third Day, and in the symbolic pageants of the *Paradiso Terrestre*. In short, we must remember that Marco's reasoning is addressed to the Pilgrim at a very specific point in his ascent; and its effect is simply to restore to the Pilgrim the use of the Natural Reason. As Marco concludes, the *lumen naturale* of the real world, the world beyond the smoke, begins to shine through. When the travellers reach it, leaving the smoke behind, Virgil with his pagan wisdom can take charge once more.

At this point I hope the reader will pause to consider the

complex unity of Canto xvi as a whole. The Pilgrim (whose consciousness is our guide) is in close darkness, but trying to release himself from it by means of the one faculty he can use, the discursive reason. The paradoxes of the discursive reason, in its effort to grasp human life univocally, have the same effect as the smoke: they bind the soul to "one of its faculties," and so divide it. This condition is first felt in the individual soul, which cannot comprehend its freedom and responsibility univocally, and then in society, whose rulers, greedy for material things and thinking in absolute either-or terms, darken and divide society. By rehearsing all this we resuffer the frustrations of anger; but we do so, not as the end of our effort, but as a means of going farther; for Marco, in the very act of presenting the tragedy, leads us to other uses of the mind and other directions of the spirit. When the Pilgrim has been through this process, the situation is seen in a new way (literally a "new light") and the canto ends. The canto is thus a little drama with a beginning, middle, and end; an act in the Pilgrim's drama of spiritual growth. It has the "form of moral growth" which we studied in Chapter II. That is, the Pilgrim is following the sequence *poiema—pathema—mathema,* but his "poiema"—what he tries to *do* here—is essentially intellectual. For this reason, neither the "suffering" (*pathema*) nor the "knowledge" (*mathema*) is much developed; they will be in the next canto. The "doing" part of the learning process on the other hand—the mental effort of the Pilgrim—is developed as an Agon, or struggle, of several kinds. In the foreground is Marco's dialectic; in the background the relentless collisions of the ruling powers of Italy. As the new light dawns these struggles are transcended, and the Pilgrim is made ready to suffer the wider insights which Virgil has to offer in Canto xvii.

The basic situation of Canto xvi—the human struggle, with the divisive arms of the discursive reason, in thick darkness—is, I think, very familiar to us in the modern

world. It has been expounded by thinkers of various persuasions, traced in the atomization of our conception of the
human; in the dissolution of our traditional culture and education; in the anarchy of our societies and the growing
relentlessness of our wars. We live in a hell of mutually-
exclusive rationalizations. And I believe that Canto xvi, if
carefully read, can help one to understand this plight.

I suppose it was in the 17th century, the heroic age of the
Enlightenment, that the Reason of Plato and Aristotle, the
lumen naturale of the Middle Ages, was finally lost, and replaced by *la raison*, "reason" limited to the myopic rigors of
geometry. In the two cantos we have been considering, xv
and xvi, Dante was apparently picturing a mode of the
spirit's life closely analogous to that of the Neoclassic, or
Rationalistic, or Baroque 17th century. His use of sharp
chiaroscuro, the blaze of light in Canto xv, the blackness of
Canto xvi, "feels like" a great deal of Baroque painting. And
it expresses a similar rationalized, oversimplified, and sensa-
tional split in the soul and the soul's understanding. Sometimes this split appears to be between earth and heaven: the
Baroque saints, impotently writhing upward, show it that
way, and Dante, as we have seen, presents the first glare of
the mind's light as a premonition of heaven, and the ensuing
darkness of earth as *buio d'inferno*, "darkness of hell"—as
though the intermediate realms of the natural world and of
purgatory did not exist. Sometimes, as in Racine, the split is
supposed to be between "reason" and passion, and this formu-
lation is close to the Pilgrim's, when he first questions Marco.
Pascal is the great master of this split, and it would be interesting to compare his passionate and reasoned struggle with
the darkness of his times with Dante's drama-of-the-mind in
this sequence. But such analogies as these would lead us too
far afield, and I mention them here merely as suggestions for
the reader of good will to mull over.

These analogies, moreover, since they *are* analogies and
not identities, must be handled with care. Other parts of the

Purgatorio are also analogous to certain phases of the Rationalistic experience, as I shall point out below. And, most important, Dante presents the plight of his Pilgrim here, not *à la* Racine or Pascal, as the ultimate reality of the human situation, but as one phase in the soul's growth. He shows the splits of the growing soul with incomparable depth, but in doing so he does not lose his sanity, his wider perspective. And in the next canto he will show human life in another light altogether: the *lumen naturale* as it returns to the Pilgrim when he is purged of anger, and freed from the absolutism of the discursive reason.

🎵 CHAPTER 10. CANTO XVII: THE ANALOGOUS FORMS OF HUMAN LOVES

CANTO XVII begins with the dissolving of the smoke of Anger through which the travellers had so painfully struggled. The effect, we are told, is like the melting of a thick mist in high mountain-country, when the sun feebly begins to reappear. As the Pilgrim emerges into the evening light (for the sun is now near setting), he can see the Anger he has transcended imaged in the mind's eye as Procne, Haman, and Amata. These waking-dreams of the angry absorb him completely, one by one, forming like "bubbles" and then dissolving as bubbles burst, when the water of which they are made "fails." The bubble-image is consonant with the image of mist dispersing in sunlight, which thus dominates the opening sequence, to line 40, when the Pilgrim is wakened to his immediate situation by the light of the angel of the stair. The travellers proceed to climb to the next terrace, where Sloth is purged, as the rays of the sun, moving higher up the Mountain, leave them in darkness here. On this Mountain one cannot go upward when darkness falls, and the travellers feel their strength depart, coming to rest like a ship that is berthed.

This sequence, approximately the first half of the canto, is immediately intelligible as the return to the real world from the smoke, which felt, not like a natural mist, but hellish and artificial, when we first met it. It also conveys, with great psychological accuracy, the experience of recovering from a fit of anger: the relief one feels as the congestion dissolves, and the familiar world looks real again; the insights into one's own spirit which come at such a time; the relaxation, and the failure of strength.

The Pilgrim, as usual, is reaping the fruit of wider understanding which always comes after the effort and suffering of each terrace. But his access of understanding is greater than ever before. The height of the Mountain, at this point, suggests that; and the Pilgrim has a new appreciation of the meaning of his day-dream images for the whole purgatorial journey. Dante introduces them by a triumphant exclamation, which he interpolates as author (line 13):

> O immaginativa, che ne rube
> tal volta sì di fuor, ch'uom non s'accorge,
> perchè d'intorno suonin mille tube,
> chi move te, se il senso non ti porge?
> Moveti lume, che nel ciel s'informa
> per sè, o per voler che giù lo scorge.

> (O imagination, that can so rob us
> out of ourselves, that we are unaware,
> although a thousand trumpets sound about us,
> who moves you, if no touch of sense is there?
> a light moves you, formed in heaven, of itself
> or by a will that downward aims its flare.)

And when the light of the angel of the stair, who invites them to ascend, overwhelms the Pilgrim as before, Virgil can reassure him in a very significant phrase (line 58):

> "Sì fa con noi, come l'uom si fa sego"

> ("He deals with us as man must deal with man")

Such images and formulations as these converge to remind us of the purpose of our journey—to reach "the better," as the first line of the *Purgatorio* has told us. And they encourage us to feel that we are coming closer. The visions which our imagination forms, of various postures of the human psyche, ancient or mythic, or recent or historic, though not directly from the senses, have their meaning and their heavenly truth. The obligation, or command, to ascend is now close to our own impulse. In terms of the literal story of the climb, the ascent grows ever easier; in terms of the Pilgrim's action, his will is more consonant with the Good, the goal of his climb: he experiences the truth of Marco's formula for the freedom of the will (Canto xvi, line 79):

> "A maggior forza ed a miglior natura
> liberi soggiacete,"

> ("To greater power and a better nature
> you are subject, in your freedom,")

In short, the Pilgrim's new freedom and understanding at this point is the fruit, not only of his transcendence of anger, but of his labors and sufferings through the whole journey up to this point. Canto xvii (with the first part of Canto xviii) is one of the great centers of understanding of the whole poem: one of the places in which the Pilgrim can grasp the nature of the drama of purgation by analogy with his own knowledge of himself.

Canto xvii may be recognized as important for the understanding of the whole poem, from several points of view. It is, for example, half-way between the Dark Wood, in which the whole *Commedia* begins, and the final ineffable vision with which the *Paradiso* ends; Dante, as was his custom, indicates the importance of this canto arithmetically. Moreover, Virgil's discourse on the forms of human love which occupies the whole second half of the canto is the best place in which to study the abstract ethical schemes which Dante used in constructing the *Purgatorio*. The classification of sins, from Pride at the bottom to Lust at the top, is here briefly set forth and theoretically justified. And this canto, with the first part of the next, marks the climax of Virgil's guidance, training and teaching, which began at the threshold of Hell; for after Canto xviii, as I have remarked above, Virgil forms a third with Statius and the Pilgrim, until Beatrice herself appears.

I wish to consider Virgil's discourse as the end, or "epiphany," of the drama of the second Day: the Pilgrim's quest, first morally, then intellectually, for the Good, with Virgil's *lumen naturale* as guide. In order to bring out the dramatic value of Virgil's discourse—the context which is a large part of its "meaning"—perhaps the following diagram may help.

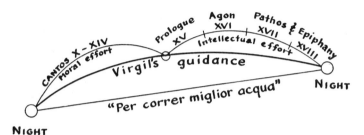

The straight ascending line at the bottom, labelled with the first line of the *Purgatorio*, represents the continuing movement which is below the Pilgrim's awareness. The next ascending curve, a heavy line, represents the movement of the second Day, the struggle upward under Virgil's guidance. This movement has two main developments, the moral effort of Cantos x-xiv, and the intellectual effort of Cantos xv-xviii. At the top I have indicated the "acts" of the intellectual drama: Canto xv, which is a prologue, setting the stage and suggesting the issues; Canto xvi, an Agon or struggle; and Canto xvii, when the results of the struggle are suffered as visions, and the true and transcendent understanding of it emerges: the "pathos and epiphany" of that drama. Canto xviii, as I shall explain in the next chapter, is both part of the epiphany of the mind's drama, when the Pilgrim pauses to enjoy the intellectual vision of love, and also the dissolution of that vision, as night gradually wipes out his waking concentration.

There are three circles on this diagram, representing important moments of transition, when the Pilgrim's immediate motivation changes in response to a new sense of the soul's potentialities. The two which are respectively at the bottom and at the top of the diagram represent the nights which bound the second Day. The Pilgrim has no immediate motivation; at night the "direction" of his soul, under Faith, Hope, and Charity, coincides with the continuing underlying aspiration of the whole journey. The circle in the center, including the end of Canto xiv and the beginning of Canto xv, represents the shift from moral to intellectual effort. It is a return to the main movement, or theme, of the whole Day, the following of Virgil's *lumen naturale*, which at that point is suddenly felt to reveal very wide perspectives.

It will be noticed that in Canto xvii the line representing the Pilgrim's immediate action or *moto spiritale* begins to approach the line representing the basic motivation of the whole Day. That is meant to indicate that at this point he almost *understands* (as distinguished from merely following) Virgil's guidance.

But to return to that moment in Canto xvii (line 76) when the Pilgrim and his guide can go no farther and prepare to enjoy the fruit of understanding they have earned. The light of the sun is far above them; they are in shadow and silence on this height; and when Virgil has explained that on this terrace Sloth is purged, he starts his great discourse in these words (line 91):

> "Nè creator nè creatura mai,"
> cominciò ei, "figliuol, fu senza amore,
> o naturale o d'animo; e tu il sai."

> ("Neither creator nor created being,"
> he began, "my son, was ever without love,
> nature's or spirit's, and that you see.")

The Pilgrim knows, says Virgil, that every creature, like the Creator, is moved by love. He knows this because he has just felt *and* perceived his own love move him up the stairs in response to the divine light and the words of the third

Beatitude, *Beati pacifici*: coming closer (as the diagram indicates) to his own deepest motivation, he "knows" both it and its goal more clearly than ever before. Moreover, he knows it because, having emerged from anger and the confinement of his own mind, he can be aware, not only mentally but by a sympathetic response of his whole being, of the vast world of creatures, all vaguely moved by love toward what seems good to them.

It is true that the mountain-height where the travellers are pausing is silent, empty, and sinking into dusk. The Pilgrim does not see the world of creatures with the physical eye. But Virgil (as he continues his discourse) appeals to the perceptions stored in the Pilgrim's memory; today's experience of the repentant Proud, Envious, and Angry (lines 115-126), and even the experience of the distorted loves, the *impasses*, of Hell (lines 100-102). The reader also, as he mulls over Virgil's words, should remember the movement of the whole journey. He should try to grasp it as a *moto spiritale*, the ever-changing movement of human love in response to evil, or good, or better—to real or illusory—objects. It is of course the Pilgrim's moving love which gives unity and continuity to the whole.

If the reader will refer once more to the diagram, he will see that the explorations which the Pilgrim makes, by sympathetic identification, of the distorted loves of the Proud, Envious, and Angry may be understood as variations upon the main theme of his own inchoate love of "the better." After each of these peripheral developments, or variations, we return to the main theme: the movement from the unformed love of the simple soul, its natural and God-given but unguided needs, through the illusions and divisions of the world, and on toward "the better" which would be its satisfaction and fulfillment. At the silent point we have now reached, the Pilgrim has made the return to the main theme so often and in so many ways that he can generalize about it: he can begin to grasp the nature of Eros, love in the human clay, the fallible aspiration of the creature toward the Good.

In Canto xxiv Dante will define his poetry, the *dolce stil nuovo*, as obedience to love. These studies assume that the *poem* which is the *Purgatorio* may be regarded as the imitation of love's varied movements. The act of composing the poem would itself be mimetic; and just as we see Dante the Pilgrim understanding the loves of the spirits he meets by a mimetic response (sym-pathy) so we may imagine Dante the author, as he makes his poem, imitating *that* response in the complex medium of language. This is not the place to examine the formula for the *dolce stil nuovo* in detail; I shall attempt it below. But this is one of the places we shall need to remember: it presents, not Dante's matured knowledge of love, but Virgil's love, or Eros, which is an essential component of it.

Virgil's discourse (lines 91-139) is so clear literally that it would be worse than futile to summarize it. Nor do I wish to repeat the labors of the commentators who, as I have remarked, derive from it the blueprints, the abstract ethical schemes, which Dante used in his construction-work. But I have a few further remarks to make upon its style of thought, the kind of insight, or knowledge, which it contains.

One might describe it, first of all, as a family tree, or genealogy, of human loves; something very like the diagram of a phylum of animal species according to a theory of evolution. The main trunk is the Pilgrim's aspiration; the branches, twigs, and leaves are the limited or misdirected loves which he explores on the way up—the dead twigs of Hell; the still-living and centrally-nourished detours of Purgatory. It is full of the sense of the kinship between all forms of life; its insights could only be those of one (Aristotle) who was both a biologist and a psychologist.

It may also be regarded as the more extended answer to the basic problem which obsessed the Pilgrim in Canto xvi. Human motivation is not to be grasped in mechanical terms, as the Pilgrim demanded in the darkness of Anger, but by analogy with other forms of life. For this purpose, Virgil appeals not to logic, but to perception; not to the mathematical or "scientific" mind, but to the whole awareness, whereby the reality and significance of other people, other creatures, reaches us. Virgil's discourse is, in short, a masterpiece of his *lumen naturale*, the mind in the real world, freed of its self-idolatries.

But, having said so much, it must be pointed out that the discourse as a whole is presented as insufficient. Though it is full of a sense of ordered life, all lives are remote: remembered, as I have said, or dim, like a view of a piece of country from a great height, when the general outlines and relationships emerge, but the actualities of the terrain, rough spots and smooth, rock and woods, are lost. It is a little ghostly, like all of Virgil's wisdom. And, as such, it takes its place within the poetic-dramatic unity of the canto as a whole, which was so clearly suggested in the opening images, especially that of the iridescent bubble which vanishes when the water which sustains it "fails." The Pilgrim, throughout, lacks the strength quite to realize the satisfaction which seems so close; the light of the world, at this height and this late hour, is not quite enough. And the whole experience of the Pilgrim, in spite of his growth in power and understanding, echoes the homesickness of the first evening, in Canto VIII.

What is lacking will be clearer in Canto XVIII. For there we shall see the Pilgrim trying to enjoy to the full what he does have: Virgil's refined and noble spirit, and Virgil's intellectual grasp of Eros, the highest form of love in the human clay.

❧ CHAPTER 11. CANTO XVIII: THE FRUIT OF PHILOSOPHY

IN THE FIRST PART of Canto XVIII, Virgil resumes and completes the discourse of love which he had begun in Canto XVII. Thus Canto XVIII contains part of the "epiphany" with which the moral-intellectual drama of the second Day ends. And the question arises why Dante chose to present Virgil's wisdom, his lore of Eros, in two separate cantos.

The first answer to this crucial question is that, in the Pilgrim's struggle up the Mountain, Virgil's wisdom is not the final goal, but only a first resting-place, a first achievement in the soul's growth; and Canto XVII shows it as goal, whereas Canto XVIII shows it as not *the* goal; hence, as inadequate to the Pilgrim's deepest needs. In Canto XVII, Virgil's wisdom appears as *terminus ad quem*; and we have seen that his knowledge of love "in the human clay" enables us to understand both the endlessly-varied modes of human existence we have seen since the dark wood, and the love which has moved us past them all to this high point in our ascent. In Canto XVIII we shall see Virgil's wisdom-of-love as *terminus a quo*. It has freed and enlightened the Pilgrim's own love, but cannot finally satisfy it; and its end is thus also the beginning of a new *moto spiritale*, to be developed during the third Day. In short, what Dante the author—the poet or dramatist—is doing in this sequence, with the most delicate and tender discriminations, is simultaneously building up and dissolving the well-loved authority of Virgil's pagan school.

In order to present Virgil's wisdom as *terminus a quo*, Dante shows a new action (or *moto spiritale*) of the Pilgrim's, and as author he takes a new breath in order to present the beginning, middle, and end of this new action. It is a good example of the importance of the canto, as a unit in Dante's dramaturgy. In Canto XVII, the Pilgrim, emerging weak but clear-eyed from the smoke of Anger, was only trying to find the strength to grasp the vast panorama which Virgil unrolled before him. In Canto xviii, on the other hand, his freed but weary spirit craves satisfaction, *delectatio*, the enjoyment of love's object. He tries to find it in the intellectual enjoyment, shared with Virgil, of Virgil's luminous concept of love-in-the-human-clay, or Eros; but because this concept is only realized in the creature at a high moment of concentration, it dissolves. The flesh in its weakness and inconstancy reasserts itself; and the canto ends, as the Pilgrim sinks to sleep, with visions of many kinds of doting which the Slothful are repenting, and which are analogous to the intellectual dotings which the Pilgrim tried to rest in at the beginning of the canto.

The opening sequence of the canto indicates, as usual, the Pilgrim's new action which the canto will develop (line 1):

> Posto avea fine al suo ragionamento
>   l'alto dottore, ed attento guardava
>   nella mia vista, s'io parea contento;
> ed io, cui nuova sete ancor frugava,
>   di fuor taceva, e dentro dicea: "Forse
>   lo troppo domandar, ch'io fo, gli grava."

> (Now the explanation had been ended
>   by the high teacher, and he was observing
>   my face, to see if I seemed contented;
> and I, who felt still a new thirst's urging,
>   was silent outwardly, within me thought:
>   "Perhaps too many questions are a burden.")

The Pilgrim has Virgil's explanation of the polymorphous moving-principle of love behind him; yet thirst, a "new thirst," still drives him. He is afraid it will offend Virgil, but Virgil always sees the *moto spiritale* behind the tiniest physical signs—the lowered eyes or the faint flush—and he proceeds to meet it and lead it forth (line 7):

> Ma quel padre verace, che s'accorse
> del timido voler che non s'apriva,
> parlando di parlare ardir mi porse.
> Ond'io: "Maestro, il mio veder s'avviva
> sì nel tuo lume, ch'io discerno chiaro
> quanto la tua ragion porti o descriva;
> però ti prego, dolce padre caro,
> che mi dimostri amore, a cui riduci
> ogni buono operare e il suo contraro."

> (But that truthful father, who had made note
> of my desire within, all closed and timid,
> made me afire to speak by what he spoke.
> I then: "Master, my sight is made so vivid
> in this, your light, that I can see clearly
> your meaning, as far as you set its limit;
> therefore, dear father, I beg you tenderly
> to show me love, to which you have reduced
> every good action and its contrary.")

This brief moment of shared understanding echoes Virgil's lines in Canto xv, the brilliant but bodiless vision with which the "drama of the mind" began (line 73):

> "e quanta gente più lassù s'intende,
> più v'è da bene amare, e più vi s'ama,
> e come specchio l'uno all'altro rende."

> ("and the more folk, up there, who comprehend,
> the more to love well, and the more love is there,
> and each one mirrors back what others send.")

The lines in Canto xv were a premonition of beatitude; the analogous moment here in Canto xviii is more actual, as the Pilgrim's desire is lured forth in Virgil's warmth and light, and teacher and pupil share, and thus increase, the intellectual enjoyment of the concept of love. It is the real but momentary summit of Virgil's *philosophia*, at once the love of wisdom and the wisdom of love. It may also be understood as the rare triumph of pedagogy: the moment when teacher and pupil are actually contemplating the same idea at the same time. It reminds one of moments in the Platonic dialogues when Socrates' careful midwifery succeeds, and some light emerges which is both his and his pupil's.

The Pilgrim apparently expects that Virgil's next words will provide the final satisfaction he craves. But Virgil knows better. He knows (having "seen") the nature of his charge's thirst, or craving; and he also knows the limitations of his own wisdom, whereby he lives in desire but without hope. He will begin his elucidation of the love he knows (Eros) with a warning that it is polymorphous, potentially evil as well as good; and in the second part of his discourse he will refer to Beatrice (as he had when the light of the mind first dawned upon the Pilgrim) for the final answer. Thus in the complex shift of perspective here presented, from Eros as *terminus ad quem* to Eros as *terminus a quo*, it is the Pilgrim who first overestimates and then loses Virgil's wisdom; Virgil himself is undeluded and truthful throughout; intact in his nobility, sadly aware of the mystery which surrounds the little area of his *lumen naturale*.

Virgil begins his great discourse with a warning not to over-estimate the love he is about to expound (line 17):

> fieti manifesto
> l'error dei ciechi che si fanno duci

> (there shall be made clear to you
> the error of the blind who would be leaders)

He then expounds love as *moto spiritale* (line 32); "movement of the spirit" toward what it perceives and finds pleasing. The human spirit is by its very nature always thus "moving," and I have used the phrase *moto spiritale* again and again in these studies, for the particular movement of spirit which a canto or a scene or a character presents. Virgil's explanation of this concept (lines 19-39 and 46-75) is the most extended general elucidation Dante ever wrote of the endlessly-varied life or movement of the human psyche: the spiritual content (the "Second Subject," as he puts it in the *Letter to Can Grande*) of the *Purgatorio* and *mutatis mutandis* of the *Inferno* and *Paradiso* as well. It should be carefully mulled-over by the reader, for it shows a great deal about the subject of Dante's poem and also about how he understood the making of the poem itself. At this point I wish to offer two observations upon it.

The first is that the notion of love as *moto spiritale* is very closely akin to Aristotle's notion of *praxis*, usually translated "action." *Praxis*, or action, also means a movement of spirit, and not the physical movements and outward deeds which result. The word "movement" is thus used analogically. Aristotle's *action*, like Dante's *moto spiritale*, is another word for the life of the human psyche: "life," says Aristotle (Butcher, *Poetics*, VI-9, p. 27) "consists in action, and its end (or goal) is a mode of action." On this notion Aristotle built up his theory of the arts as "imitations" of action, in their various media, and in various ways—imitations, not of the literal surfaces of life, but of the underlying movement of spirit. It is as imitations of the spirit's variegated life that the arts have meanings wider than that of literal fact; *general* significance akin to that of philosophic systems. Dante employs a similar conception of the poetic art when he composes his characters, stories, metaphors, and musical effects in such a way as to reveal, at a very deep level, a certain *moto spiritale*. In his poem-making, the literal texture of the poem serves, like the outward deeds of a man or the visible green leaves of a plant (lines 49-54), to reveal the life within.

Dante did not have Aristotle's *Poetics* to read, but I suppose there is no doubt that the psychology here presented—

psychology in the ancient sense of the *wisdom* of the human psyche, not in the sense of our contemporary pseudo-sciences of psychology—was based on Greek and especially Aristotelian concepts. But it would be a bad mistake to conclude that the notion of *moto spiritale* and the notion of *praxis* are identical, in spite of their similarity. Dante's generation confirmed, but amplified, deepened, and thus qualified the ancient "Soul's knowledge of itself." I shall try to suggest that below, apropos of Statius's picture of the soul's life (Canto xxv). Dante's conception of poem-making is related to Aristotle's *Poetics* in a similar way; it does not so much contradict as deepen it; and this point also I shall return to below, apropos of the formula for the *dolce stil nuovo*, in Canto xxiv. Meanwhile, I wish to return to Virgil's discourse, which presents, not Dante's final view of the soul's life, but its natural basis—more than enough to detain us here.

Virgil's elucidation of his notion of love consists of an elaborate set of analogies, and this one must understand if one is to get the *kind* of knowledge, or insight, intended here. The "family tree of human loves" of Canto xvii was analogical in its structure and relationships. Here Virgil assumes that we possess to some extent that analogical notion of human-love-in-general which is the basis of the family tree: in other words, we have that wisdom-of-love which we saw him sharing with the timid Pilgrim at the beginning of this canto. It is this notion he now proceeds to explore, by means of a different set of analogies: to physical movement, to the moving principles (or life) of growing plants, and to the life of animals. These analogies correct and amplify each other, showing the human *moto spiritale* in many complementary perspectives. The perspectives get wider and deeper as the discourse proceeds upward, from the analogies of fire and wax, through the nonsentient growth of plants, to the instinct of bees, and thence to the human psyche itself, with its freedom, awareness, self-awareness, and terrifyingly-wide potentialities—for good or evil—which are beyond the animal altogether. So we are back to *philosophia*, that mode of awareness which is Virgil's masterpiece; and his discourse ends with a reference, far ahead, to the unseen Beatrice.

There is no doubt that Dante intended this discourse, with its poetic concision and its prose-like clarity, to mark a summit of awareness. How startling, then, to read (line 76):

> La luna, quasi a mezza notte tarda,
>> facea le stelle a noi parer più rade,
>> fatta com' un secchione che tutto arda;
> e correa contra il ciel, per quelle strade
>> che il sole infiamma allor che quel da Roma
>> tra i Sardi e i Corsi il vede quando cade.
> E quell' ombra gentil, per cui si noma
>> Pietola più che villa Mantovana,
>> del mio carcar deposto avea la soma:
> per ch'io, che la ragione aperta e piana
>> sopra le mie questioni avea ricolta,
>> stava com'uom che sonnolento vana.

> (The moon, retarded almost to midnight,
>> was making the stars appear more thin to us,
>> shaped like a bucket burningly alight;
> she moved against the heavens upon the course
>> the sun inflames, when Romans mark her setting
>> between Sardinia and the Isle of Corse.
> And that gentle shadow, through whom is mentioned
>> Pietola above all Mantuan towns,
>> had now laid down the burden I had set him:
> I therefore, in his reasons having found
>> plain open answers to my questioning,
>> stood there as one who wanderingly drowsed.)

The light of the moon, which had been silently rising over our pleasure in Virgil's light, surprises us almost guiltily. But the next minute we understand that it merely brings out the other, the sinister aspect of the action of this canto, which had been implicit all along: the fact that Virgil's truth cannot satisfy the Pilgrim's new thirst, and that, if we misinterpret the finality of Virgil's achievement (as the Pilgrim slothfully tends to do) it may even be illusory. The appearance of the moon thus marks the turning-point in the action of the canto, and introduces the long movement of dissolution and fading-away which ends when the Pilgrim sinks into sleep.

The moon itself, at this point, is a fine example of Dante's symbolism, which is at once "poetic," like Shakespeare's richly suggestive metaphors, and "allegorical," in that it has also traditional and carefully thought-out meanings within Dante's whole framework of philosophy and cosmology. Thus we get it, first, reading along in all innocence, as the very moon we know, which rises over our loves and the loves of tom-cats on the back fence, disturbing us with a sense of wide, dangerous, and alluring potentialities. The moment of concentration upon the summit of *philo-sophia* is gone, and we are reminded of the more heedless loves which move the world of nature and our human clay. The moon here also plays a role like that of the moon's aurora in Canto IX, the first night of the journey: its white light announces the nightly relapse of the soul into the body, obedient to mortal weariness, the more or less willed yielding to animality, and below that to gravitation. If we remember the use which Dante makes of these metaphors throughout the poem, we may feel this nightly retreat toward sleep as an image of death, physical death and the death of the spirit which the Pilgrim saw in the ice at the bottom of the universe.

Such are the poetic or metaphorical meanings of the moon, which arise from the texture of the poem and from the literal circumstances of the fictive journey. But we should reflect also that the moon fits into the whole thought-out allegorical scheme of the poem, and that its allegorical significance reinforces and expands its more immediate poetic effect. Its position in the heavens reminds us that it is late—too late; we have talked too long here in the terrace of Sloth. Its light, inspiring and alluring though it is, is a false light compared with that of the sun lighting Rome: it is only a cold and insubstantial reflection. So, when Virgil is named at this point, he is not the *alto dottore* of the beginning of the canto, but a shadow already: *quel ombra gentil*. And in this same light of the moon, the stars which rise nightly over Purgatory, signifying Christian virtues of Faith, Hope, and Charity which indicate the proper posture of the soul during the dark hours—these stars are diminished, and seem "more thin."

I have paused so long over the moon because its appearance marks an all-important turning-point, and provides an essential comment upon the unfolding of Virgil's enlightenment, which now ends. In all of these delicately-managed shifts of perspective, Virgil himself remains nobly consistent, as the undeluded pagan sage he has been all along. The drama of spiritual change is, as always, that of the Pilgrim and of the attentive reader.

The Pilgrim, who at the beginning of the canto had been concentrated upon the intelligence of love, *intelleto d'amore*, and been (as he now feels) too satisfied thereby, rambles drowsily, and knows, by intimate sympathy, the mode of being of those who repent their sloth. The sloth which they repent is figured by their inability to go ahead, like the Pilgrim's inability to get beyond Virgil's discourse. The "whip of love" which drives them to rehearse the painful nature of their fault, looks like fanaticism—a form of love as far from Virgil's classic measure as sloth and animality itself. Thus the machinery of the purgation of those "whom good will and just love bestride" is similar in principle to the purgation of the spirits we have seen below; but here the process is more conscious and swift, as is appropriate at this more free and forewarned level of development. I do not pause over the examples of zeal and then of sloth which are quickly rehearsed, nor upon the testimony of the Abbot of San Zeno (lines 113-126), beyond pointing out the significance of the deformed son of Alberto della Scala at this point in the canto. This image echoes the "crooked going" of love, which the Pilgrim has uneasily felt in the midst of Virgil's discourse (line 45). And it foreshadows the deformed Siren of the Pilgrim's dream in the next canto, a monstrosity warmed into illusory life and attractiveness by the attention, and then the love, which the dreamer gives her. In general, the imagery of the final sequence of the canto, with its haste, its grotesquerie, and its terror, all on the background of the Pilgrim's weariness and bewilderment, presents the dissolution of Virgil's ideal image, and the sharp sense of the actual anarchic power of the many forms of love in the human clay.

But before I leave this final sequence, the rush of the driven slothful, I wish to point out the extremely significant allusion with which Dante introduces it. This allusion occurs just after we have seen the Pilgrim restlessly drowsing in the deceitful brilliance of the moon (line 91):

> E quale Ismeno già vide ed Asopo
>   lungo di sè di notte furia e calca,
>   pur che i Teban di Bacco avesser uopo:
> cotal per quel giron suo passo falca,
>   per quel ch'io vidi di color, venendo,
>   cui buon volere e giusto amor cavalca.

> (Just as Ismenus and Asopus used to see
>   along their banks a furious rout by night
>   whenever the men of Thebes felt Bacchus' need,
> So then, along that terrace, I descried,
>   coming onward, hastening their paces,
>   those whom good will and a just love bestride.)

A contemporary reader, relishing this passage in its context, may remember the chorus in Sophoclean tragedy, which also invokes Bacchus (or Dionysos) when the failure of reason and moral purpose makes them need him. In the next to the last chorus in *Antigone*, for example, when all of Creon's "reasons" have failed; when his son and his people have refused his guidance, and when, abandoning his own philosophy, he starts, too late, his love-driven race to Antigone's tomb—at this point Sophocles' Thebans invoke this god by night with a frenzy like that of Dante's slothful. In *Antigone* also the god is associated with love *outside* reason, love which may be bestial or divine; Dionysos has many names and many manifestations, in drunkenness, in inspiration, and in the solicitations of undefined passion.

Dante did not know Greek tragedy, and of course he had no notion at all of the ritual role of the chorus which modern scholarship has revealed to us. He took the allusion to the Thebans' nocturnal Bacchic rout from Statius, who has three or four noncommittal lines on it in the *Thebaid*. But the context shows that Dante understood the invocation of Dionysos with a depth undreamed of by Statius. It is another instance of Dante's uncanny ability to pick up the echoes, however faint, of ancient poetry, and to amplify them in the complex harmonies of his own great composition.

Certainly, at this point, the association of the repentant slothful with the nocturnal invocation of Dionysos adds many overtones of meaning to the end of the action of this canto. This action, as I have remarked, is one of delectation; and now that we have had the intellectual pleasure of consuming the fine fruit of *philosophia*, we realize that we are still thirsting, and still subject to the power of love in the raw. Dionysos, or Bacchus, marks the return, from the movement of reason to the underlying *tragic* movement of the purgatorial journey. And before the next daylight sequence begins, we are to suffer the prophetic dreams and the mysterious power of love as the force of both good and evil, which come, as in the Sophoclean chorus, when reason, daylight, and the moral will are unavailable.

❧ CHAPTER 12. ON INTERPRETING VIRGIL

"PHILOSOPHY," Dante wrote in the *Convivio*—"Philosophy . . . which is 'the loving exercise of wisdom,' contemplates herself when the beauty of her eyes is revealed to herself. And what else is this but to say that the philosophizing soul not only contemplates the truth, but also contemplates its own contemplation and the beauty thereof, turning upon itself and enamouring itself of itself by reason of the beauty of its direct contemplation?" This passage exactly describes the Pilgrim's experience in the terrace of the Slothful, in the evening of the second Day, when in the light of Virgil's philosophy he pauses to contemplate Eros, in its fulfillment, looking inward to enjoy the enjoyment of the perception of truth.

There is plenty of intrinsic evidence both in the *Convivio* and in the *Purgatorio* that the journey of the second Day represents Dante's final understanding of his own struggle for reason, the part of his life which culminated in his attempt to write the *Convivio*. That work was conceived in a mood of intellectual and moral confidence. It was to be a banquet of the mind to which, with Aristotelian magnanimity, he would invite his friends. He would give them the key to ancient poetry and history, to the conduct of life from the cradle to the grave, to the order of society, and to the arts and sciences. This key was philosophy: at once the sufficient end and the sufficient explanation of human life. In short, he was offering all that the Pilgrim slowly acquires during the second Day, under Virgil's guidance, as he learns to see that the path to intellectual and moral freedom is very old, and that the classics, therefore, speak directly to his experience. He was offering, as the climax of the banquet, the same pleasure of philosophic contemplation which the Pilgrim finds so briefly in Canto XVIII. The *Convivio*, therefore, and Dante's own experience in writing it and then giving it up, throws a great deal of light upon the Pilgrim's acquisition of Virgil's philosophy.

"Clearly Dante's dominating motive in writing the *Convivio*," Philip Wicksteed writes "was a passion for the study and the promulgation of philosophic truth." That, he goes on to say, was not a matter of Dante's formal adherence to the Church, which never wavered; it was a matter of his own actual inner life, then focussed in the reason. After he turned away from the *Vita Nuova* and the love for Beatrice which it celebrates, he plunged into the life of the citizen on the way to his marvellous maturity: he engaged in politics, war, learning, love and thought; he wrote, among other things, his *Odes*, which are inspired by secular loves quite unlike the love of the *Vita Nuova*. The *Convivio* is an attempt to rationalize both his life and his writings up to that moment. The attempt, for all its power and intelligence, failed; he abandoned the *Convivio* without finishing it.

The nature of this partial failure may be most clearly seen in the *Convivio* itself, in his attempt to allegorize his own *Odes*. If he was to be the perfect sage, obedient only to reason, then, as he frankly says, he will have to clear himself of "the infamy of having yielded to so great a passion" as the *Odes* seem to present. For this purpose he offers a theory of poetry, which he calls the "allegory of poets," according to which poetry is merely illustrative of the concepts of moral philosophy: "As when Ovid says that Orpheus with his lyre made wild beasts tame and made trees and rocks approach him; which would say that the wise man with the instrument of his voice maketh cruel hearts tender and humble." In this theory, it is clear, the authority of philosophy is affirmed; but the concrete actuality of the poem and its unique insight, is denied. Armed with this theory, Dante then tries to allegorize his *Odes* by interpreting the woman to whom they are addressed as "My Lady Philosophy." It is probable that some of the *Odes* are indeed poems of philosophic contemplation, but others are unmistakably addressed to a woman of flesh and blood: they are among the most cruelly passionate love-poems in the tradition. They prove stronger than philosophy: it would be clear to any reader that *Ode VI*, for instance (which Dante never reached in his allegorizing) presents a mode of being, a direction of love, which cannot be rationalized away, and which is not aiming toward reason.

The struggle which one may dimly make out behind the writing and the abandonment of the *Convivio* is very moving. One cannot doubt the reality of Dante's craving for reason, nor the knowledge and wisdom it brought him. At the same time the *Odes* are there, testifying to the non-rational depths of Dante's passional life, to his knowledge of it, and to his mastery of the art of representing it. He could not get the two aspects of his experience into focus together; when he tried, they falsified each other.

In recent years we have witnessed some impressive efforts to build an all-sufficing philosophy like Virgil's, or like that of the *Convivio*: an affirmation of humane reason and of the timeless validity of its classic achievements. The recurrent attempt to restore a liberal curriculum in our universities is one of these; Erskine's reforms at Columbia after the first World War, Hutchins' curriculum at Chicago, the St. Johns great-books project (the most radical effort of all to feed the mind its favorite food), mark the course of this noble cult of reason in the ancient sense. Irving Babbit's Humanism, which stirred up a brief but violent controversy in the early 'thirties, was a related attempt. The attacks on these movements were made in the name of Progressive Education, or Freud, or modern art and literature, the vast lore of the actual, passion-driven lives of the modern world. The political analogue of the return to the humane tradition in education and morals is the "liberal center," which seeks to preserve the humane and more or less rationalized values embodied in constitutional government in the face of swift change. The criticism of political liberalism has been practical: it is to be found in the destructive power of non-rational totalitarian creeds. Such contemporary issues as these reflect the same paradoxical nature of reason and its timeless truths which Dante encountered when he tried to follow the plan of the *Convivio* to its logical conclusion. The nowhere of abstract truth alternates with the nowhere of the world without reason.

Perhaps it was when Dante abandoned the *Convivio* that he had his vision of Hell, where the good of the intellect is lost. The Pilgrim in his struggle to learn Virgil's philosophy feels the threat of Hell whenever his reason fails for the moment—in the darkness of anger, for instance, or in the inspired fanaticism of the repentant slothful under the moon. But Dante the author, who devised the drama of the mind in which Virgil leads the Pilgrim into the world of reason and out again, no longer either deified reason or despaired of it. He saw how to represent the indispensable life of reason with due regard for its authority and also its limitations: as only a mode of the life of the psyche, and as a stage in its growth.

Thus the concrete, dramatic style of the *Purgatorio*, contrasting sharply with the abstract and rational style of the *Convivio*, itself shows how Dante understood reason and Virgil's philosophy. The style of the *Convivio* sacrifices everything to the demands of reason: Dante himself, as he writes it, is hardly distinguishable from the "Master of those who know"; the historic life of the past, ancient poetry, Dante's own poetry and his life up to that point, are all reduced to mere illustrations of rational principles. But in the *Purgatorio* Dante is seen as the Pilgrim who learns, errs, and changes before our eyes. The historic or legendary lives of the past appear visibly or speak audibly, with an impact as of real people. Virgil represents reason and philosophy, not as a personification of reason, but as a particular spirit who uses reason, and teaches its use to the Pilgrim. Thus in the style itself the demands of the poetic imagination for the concrete and actual are recognized. The life of reason is seen *within* the individual spirits of Virgil and the Pilgrim, and in their communion; and when it flickers out for the night, Virgil and the Pilgrim are left in the wider scene of the Mountain, a reflection of the real world. In the *Convivio*, when reason fails, nothing is left.

When Dante wrote the *Convivio* he was trying to think of poetry in terms of his "allegory of poets"; when he wrote the *Commedia* he conceived his poem-making in terms of the "allegory of theologians," as he explains to Can Grande. He was no longer trying to make his style obedient to reason only; he had a still more ambitious purpose and criterion: to make it obedient to God as revealed in Christianity. He wanted to make a poem which would be true as he believed Scripture was true. He wanted it to reflect the drama of man's life in the real world, in actual history, and in hidden but perpetual relation to God, as the Christian faith sees that drama. Thus in the *Commedia* a cosmic and historic drama replaces the abstract truths of reason as the ultimate meaning of the poem, and a dramatic conception of form replaces rationality as the basis of its style, or art.

When Dante the Pilgrim sees that Virgil's philosophy is not reality itself, he is ready to begin to understand Virgil *himself*, and his role in the drama of his own progress. The Pilgrim is like a young man who, in the process of growing up, comes to see his father, not as a timeless presence of unknown scope and limitless knowledge, but as a limited and fallible human being. The reader, following the Pilgrim, can now begin to "interpret" Virgil, in accordance with Dante's principle, "the interpretation of the Letter is the development of the form." The Pilgrim has acquired Virgil's wisdom, he has been initiated into the timeless society of pagan sages. And now, during the third Day, with Virgil and Statius, he will live the life of humane reason, and at last come to its end, as Beatrice appears. She comes, in the *Paradiso Terrestre*, with the pageant which unrolls the Christian drama of man's earthly life in history. And the reader, looking through the Pilgrim's eyes and then thinking about what he has seen, can interpret Virgil's philosophy within that historic drama.

The purpose of these observations, however, is not to complete the interpretation of Virgil. I only wish to point out what the process of interpreting his meaning should be: not rationalistic allegorizing, but close attention to his ever-developing role in the poem. His strong and gentle spirit accompanies the Pilgrim about two-thirds of the way from Hell to the final vision of God. The dawning of his enlightenment in the middle of the *Purgatorio* is one of the great centers of understanding in the whole journey. Even in the *Paradiso* the justice and reason he taught the Pilgrim is reaffirmed; and the poem itself was made possible by the philosophic and literary culture he brought. But because Dante thought that he owed his escape from Hell to Virgil and his reason, he went on to enquire, to what did he owe Virgil? What caused the rebirth, in his time and in his own spirit, of the ancient wisdom? How did the life of reason, so ghostly on the printed page, and in the solitude of the reading-lamp, acquire once more a certain life in men and in time? Such questions as these underlie the journey of the third Day, when the interpretation of Virgil is gently and tragically completed.

PART THREE

THE PILGRIM AGAINST TIME
(THE THIRD DAY: CANTOS XIX-XXVII)

THE STORY of the Pilgrim's journey from the foot of the Mountain to a point high on its flank, has shown us the general meaning of the new scene which opens before him on the third Day. Dante, a medieval Italian, has achieved the freedom and understanding of Virgil's ancient wisdom; he is now a member of the ideal society of pagan sages. He and Virgil will soon be joined by Statius, the Roman poet who, Dante believed, had been converted late in life to Christianity. It is as though the rendezvous were in Augustan Rome, a crossroads of pagan and Christian culture. But it is not that literally; it is only the spirits of Virgil and Statius that the Pilgrim meets. The scene represents the height of human awareness, the life of reason: the goal of free spirits in any generation; the realm, which proves rather ghostly, of timeless humanism.

The story of the third Day itself will recount the Pilgrim's visions of the repentant avaricious, greedy and lustful. The very freedom of the spirit at this high point makes it sensitive to the good things of earth; but its moral sophistication reveals the inadequacy of these delights almost as soon as their attractiveness is felt. That is clearly foreseen in the dream of the Siren (Canto XIX) which the Pilgrim has just before the third Day dawns. The Siren looks ugly when he first sees her, but his love, lacking an object which would finally satisfy it, turns toward her. Under his gaze she is warmed into life and beauty as night-chilled limbs are warmed by the sun, and presently she is "colored as love wills." At the very moment of pleasure a "holy lady" appears, who scolds Virgil for allowing his charge to yield to the ancient temptation, and Virgil rips open her clothes, revealing the belly, and the stench wakes the Pilgrim. The difference between this dream and that of the first night (Canto IX) shows how far the Pilgrim has come. His eroticism is now that of the mature male; moreover, he knows what it means. Virgil himself appears in the dream; Virgil's wisdom is now in his own spirit.

The distance which the Pilgrim will traverse during the third Day is indicated in the literal story of the *Commedia* as a whole. He will climb from the point where Virgil's light dawned on him to the point (Eden) where Beatrice will appear. He is thus approaching the end and the cause of the whole journey. We learned in the beginning of the *Inferno* that Beatrice had sent Virgil to bring the Pilgrim back to her; her unseen love has therefore been behind the Pilgrim's love for Virgil and his wisdom all along. As Dante the man returned, after his attempt to write the *Convivio*, from My Lady Philosophy to his earliest intimations of love, and saw it, then, as of unimaginable depth and meaning, so now the Pilgrim returns to Beatrice, to find her more wonderful and terrifying than he knew.

The Pilgrim knows what the reader of the *Commedia* up to this point knows, but no more. He does not know what it will require to cover the rest of the distance to Beatrice. He must, as always, explore the high and mysterious realm slowly, for the first time; and it is his exploration which the reader must learn to share.

The Pilgrim feels the motive to ascend strong within him, but he does not understand it. He calls it "thirst"—that "new thirst" which he felt first (Canto xviii, line 4) when he considered his *moto spiritale* in Virgil's light, and understood it as the polymorphous love that moves the human clay. During the third Day he is not primarily trying to understand himself, but to satisfy this thirst. During the second Day he learned to understand the life of the human psyche in general terms; now he will experience its destiny in the world, and especially in history. During the second Day all that he saw and heard turned him inward, to contemplate his inner being; during the third Day he turns outward again, seeking satisfaction for his thirst—seeking Beatrice, as he believes, and, in effect, finding in this realm of high humane awareness a sense of history, his own and humanity's.

Dante indicates the nature of the Pilgrim's *moto spiritale*— a movement of faith rather than an effort of understanding— by sensuous metaphors which are quite different from the imagery of light and dark which dominates the end of the second Day. The most important are metaphors of eating and drinking; of nourishment, fattening, and thinning, based on analogies between the appetites of the spirit and the classic appetites of the flesh for money, food, and erotic satisfaction. This sequence is accompanied by another set of metaphors of climbing with great speed—sensations of lightness and height.

When the Pilgrim awakens after the dream of the Siren (Canto xix) he feels lighter, freer, and swifter than before; and this is conveyed by the analogy of the flight of birds, or of preparation for flight. The angel of the stair invites the travellers to ascend (line 46):

> Con l'ali aperte che parean di cigno,
>   volseci in su colui che sì parlonne,
>   tra' due pareti del duro macigno.

> (With wings outspread like the wings of a swan,
>   he turned us upward who thus spoke to us,
>   between the two walls of the rock-hard stone.)

In line 64 the image of flight is resumed and applied directly to the Pilgrim's *moto spiritale*:

> Quale il falcon che prima ai piè si mira,
>   indi si volge al grido, e si protende
>   per lo disio del pasto che là il tira:
> tal mi fec'io.

> (Like the falcon who glances at his feet,
>   then turns him toward the call, and spreads his wings

with the desire that draws him toward his meat:
such I became.)

When we meet Pope Adrian, pressing the earth in his repentance for his avarice, this pressure is felt as the preparation
for ascent, as his words to the Pilgrim suggest (line 133):

"Drizza le gambe, levati su, frate,"

("Straighten your legs, lift yourself up, my brother,")

This imagery refers back to Cantos XIV and XV, when the
upward call was associated with the light of the mind, and
ahead to Canto XXV, a passage along the edge of a great
height.

The phrase which I have used as a title for Part Three,
"The Pilgrim Against Time," is intended to indicate the
nature and direction of his life here. He is against time because of the impatient drive of his freed and unsatisfied love;
the haste which is felt at the very beginning of the day in
the flight-metaphors. He is against the temporal in general,
the good things of earth which, like the repentant spirits of
this realm, he desires and renounces almost at once. His communion with the ancient poets is against time, for the three
never met in the flesh, and the Pilgrim hears and sees Virgil
and Statius across a thousand years of history. The Pilgrim,
in his own spirit, is going against the temporal sequence of
his own life: he is returning to the love which Beatrice
showed him in childhood, refinding his end in his beginning.
Such is the course of the Day's climb as the Pilgrim experiences it, and as the reader may get it from the literal story
and the music and imagery of the verse.

But the Pilgrim's exploration of the high humane awareness has a meaning for every man, which he hardly understands; a meaning which Dante the author has built into
the scene and the structure of the drama. The Pilgrim's
course under Virgil's guidance, from Virgil's wisdom to his

own vision of Love in Beatrice, is a figure of the course of history from pagan antiquity to the Incarnation, which occurred under the humane rule of Rome. And because the Incarnation gives history its meaning, the Pilgrim's course is a figure of the path by which every man, in every age, must find his individual way. Everything the Pilgrim sees and hears during the third Day both confirms Virgil's wisdom and also points to the hidden Christ, the clue to history in every sense: the actual course of temporal human life.

This half-hidden Christian theme is introduced in Canto xx, the opening tercet:

> Contra miglior voler voler mal pugna:
>   onde contra il piacer mio, per piacerli,
>   trassi dell'acqua non sazia la spugna.

> (Against a better will the will fights ill:
>   against my pleasure, then, to pleasure him,
>   I from the water drew the sponge unfilled.)

These lines refer literally to the end of Canto xix, when the Pilgrim, obeying Virgil, broke off his conversation with Pope Adrian. They accurately describe that swift alternation of pleasure, renunciation, and halfwilled obedience which will mark the Pilgrim's struggle with his insatiable thirst all day. But the reader who is forewarned of the Christian theme will recognize, in the sponge image, a reference to Christ's obedience on the Cross, and see in the Pilgrim's tiny sacrifice an image of the Divine Pattern which, in Dante's scheme, underlies the whole movement of the journey. At the end of the canto the theme is more clearly announced in the tremor which shakes the Mountain, interrupting the climb (line 127):

> quand'io senti', come cosa che cada,
>   tremar lo monte: onde mi prese un gelo,
>   qual prender suol colui che a morte vada.

Certo non si scotea sì forte Delo,
    pria che Latona in lei facesse il nido
    a partorir li due occhi del cielo.
Poi cominciò da tutte parti un grido
    tal che il maestro in ver di me si feo,
    dicendo: "Non dubbiar, mentr'io ti guido."
"Gloria in excelsis," tutti, *"Deo,"*
    dicean, per quel ch'io da' vicin compresi,
    onde intender lo grido si poteo.
Noi ci restammo immobili e sospesi,
    come i pastor che prima udir quel canto,
    fin che il tremar cessò, ed ei compièsi.
Poi ripigliammo nostro cammin santo,
    guardando l'ombre che giacean per terra,
    tornate già in su l'usato pianto.
Nulla ignoranza mai con tanta guerra
    mi fe' desideroso di sapere,
    se la memoria mia in ciò non erra,
quanta pare'mi allor pensando avere;
    nè per la fretta domandarn'er'oso,
    nè per me lì potea cosa vedere:
    così m'andava timido e pensoso.

(when I felt, like something that is falling,
    the mountain shake, and then a chill of ice
    gripped me, like that which grips one toward death
    walking.
Not Delos, surely, trembled in such vise
    before Latona therein made her nest,
    when she was brought to birth of heaven's two eyes.
And then upon all sides a shout commenced
    which made the master turn him and approach,
    saying, "have no fear, while you have my behest."
"Gloria in Excelsis Deo," those
    voices all were saying, as I made out
    from those I clearly heard, which were most close.

We stood there without moving and in doubt,
    like the shepherds who first heard that singing,
    till the quake ceased, and the song faded out.
Then we resumed our holy way, observing
    the shadows that lay prone upon the earth,
    returned already to their wonted mourning.
I never felt before such painful dearth
    of understanding, nor such desire to know,
    if in this matter memory does not err,
as I then, pondering, appeared to hold;
    yet in our haste I did not dare to question,
    and there was nothing I could see alone:
    so I walked onward, timid still and pensive.)

The Pilgrim first associates the earthquake with that which
accompanied the birth of Apollo and Diana, "heaven's two
eyes." Then he recognizes the singing which follows the
tremor: the very song the shepherds heard on the night of
Christ's birth. The Pilgrim had assumed, no doubt, that his
journey was in accord with Christian philosophy and the
Creed. But merely formal knowledge never avails for the
actual life of his spirit; and at this point he cannot connect
his Christian theory with what is happening to him. He does
not know (what he will discover in the next canto) that
the shaking of the Mountain and the hymn mark the rising
of Statius, his first Christian guide, from his long repentance.
He does not know that all the people he meets here are
figures of the risen Christ. He experiences this moment of
transition, with its deathly chill, its hope, and its mystery, but
he cannot fathom it. So he will continue during the whole
third Day. He lives deeply and swiftly: with Virgil in the
light of reason, yet also at that sensitive edge of consciousness,
where all that surrounds him seems to have a meaning beyond what Virgil understands.

    The poetic and dramatic style of this part of the *Purgatorio*
—urbane, light, swift, yet full of undeveloped allusions and

implications—imitates, as always, the Pilgrim's awareness. It is a difficult style, in spite of its many beauties in the detail. It is particularly difficult for the modern reader, for we are not used to the medieval combination of realism and symbolism, nor to the theory of the symbolic, or "figural" meaning of history upon which it is based. I shall have more to say of these matters below, following the Pilgrim, whose awareness gradually approaches the Author's as the journey and the poem come to the end together.

By way of preliminary clue, I only wish to observe that Dante the author, the Christian dramatist, has half-hidden the figure of Christ, coming, or on the Cross, or risen, behind all the visible scenes of the third Day's journey. And he has placed the love of Christ, like an unseen magnet, behind the "new thirst" which drives the Pilgrim here: the source of the rebirth of ancient wisdom in Dante's time, and also of the poem which is a visible sign of that rebirth.

A GHOSTLY SCENE OF RECOGNITION

CANTO XXI shows the mysterious meeting with Statius which was prepared for by the shaking of the Mountain, and the hymn, with which Canto XX ended. The conversation between Virgil and Statius, with the Pilgrim as passionate spectator, is light and urbane, even humorous in moments. But the occasion of this meeting, high on the Mountain, of spirits widely separated by time, place, and all the conditions of mortality, gives it a deep though hidden pathos.

The canto consists chiefly of the dialogue of Virgil and Statius, with stage-directions which enable us to follow the Pilgrim's growing understanding of the scene between the two ancient sages. The Pilgrim hopes, through what Virgil and Statius reveal to each other, to satisfy that thirst which drives him onward. And the canto as a whole is what the Greeks would have called a complex Recognition Scene, with an implied Peripeteia. It consists of a prologue and four small acts, or movements, marking the stages of Virgil's and Statius' gradual recognition of each other. This is also a recognition of the situation in which they find themselves— between time gone and time redeemed, as one might put it. The canto is a particularly clear instance of the essentially dramatic form of the journey; and a little study of it throws much light on the paradoxical *moto spiritale* of the third Day, the transition, with Statius' help, from Virgil's guidance to the first appearance of Beatrice.

The prologue consists of the first thirteen lines:

> La sete natural che mai non sazia,
>> se non con l'acqua onde la femminetta
>> Samaritana domandò la grazia,
> mi travagliava, e pungeami la fretta
>> per la impacciata via retro al mio duca,
>> e condoleami alla giusta vendetta;

ed ecco, sì come ne scrive Luca
    che Christo apparve ai due ch'erano in via,
    già surto fuor della sepulcral buca,
ci apparve un'ombra, e retro a noi venia
    da piè guardando la turba che giace;
    nè ci addemmo di lei, sì parlò pria,
dicendo: "Frati miei, Dio vi dea pace."

(The natural thirst which nothing ever sates,
    except that water which the woman of
    Samaria demanded as a grace,
was working in me, with haste's goading, on
    behind my leader, up the cumbered route,
    and I was mourning the just punishment;
and see! just as Luke writes that to the two
    who were upon the way, there appeared Christ,
    new-risen from the cave-mouth of the tomb,
to us appeared a shadow, coming behind,
    gazing at the crowd that lay at its feet;
    nor did we see it, till it first made sign,
saying: "My brothers, may God give you peace.")

The ceaseless movement of this long sentence, packed with rich allusions which I do not pause to develop, presents the swift, sensitive, but unintellectual movement of the Pilgrim's inner being. This movement ends, for the moment, with Statius' appearance, which immediately absorbs the attention of the Pilgrim and Virgil. But the allusions are important, for they suggest the metaphysical scene and situation of the little play which is to follow.

Thus the Pilgrim's thirst, likened to that of the Samaritan woman, is for the first time presented in a Christian context. When he mourns the "just punishment" he is referring literally to the punishment of the avaricious which he has just seen; but we know from the *Paradiso* that Dante believed that Christ's Crucifixion, under the just rule of Rome, was just in terms of human reason and order, though with regard to the Son of God it was to be understood, not in terms of justice, but in terms of love. We are, in fact, at this point in the journey, in that situation in individual development, and also in the historic life of humanity, when the love of God appeared to judge and be judged by the highest human reason. So we are ready for Statius, both pagan sage and (as Dante believed) Christian convert; and his rising from his long repentance is associated with Christ's rising as its "type" or shadow. He becomes for Virgil and the Pilgrim the sign of "the third who walks always beside you," as Eliot puts the experience of the disciples on the road to Emmaus.

But, as I said, the Pilgrim does not pause to explore the meaning of what he senses at the edge of his awareness. Statius speaks; and the prologue, the adumbration of the situation and its issues, gives place without a break to the first act of the play.

The first act of recognition is presented in lines 14-24. It is a courteous dialogue between Virgil and Statius, in which Virgil, who wishes to know who Statius is, first identifies himself and the Pilgrim in very general terms. Virgil identifies himself as "in eternal exile," the Pilgrim as still on the thread of his mortal life, and he explains that both of them are here by a special grace, whereby Virgil guides the Pilgrim in this realm where he alone cannot see his way. And then at last he asks Statius to explain the shaking of the Mountain and the hymn.

That is the end of the first movement, and it is marked by a return to the main action, i.e., to the Pilgrim and his thirst (line 37):

> Sì mi diè domandando per la cruna
> del mio disio, che pur con la speranza
> si fece la mia sete men digiuna.

(So asking he pierced the very needle's eye
of my desire, and by hope alone
rendered my thirst less fasting and less dry.)

The next act or movement (lines 40-72) is Statius' first
identification of himself, but in terms as impersonal as those
Virgil had used. He has just risen from his long repentance,
and whenever this occurs, the Mountain shakes and the
hymn of joy is heard. But, to make this clear, Statius first
explains the nature of the Mountain itself, and then the nature of the release from repentance. All of this throws a new
light on both the action and the scene of purgation.

He expounds the meaning of the scene of purgation by
the beautiful metaphor of a Mountain height above the
earthly weather (line 40 ff.):

Quei cominciò: "Cosa non è che sanza
  ordine senta la religione
  della montagna, o che sia fuor d'usanza.
Libero è qui da ogni alterazione;
  di quel che il ciel da sè in sè riceve
  esserci puote, e non d'altro, cagione:
perchè non pioggia, non grando, non neve,
  non rugiada, non brina più su cade
  che la scaletta dei tre gradi breve.
Nuvole spesse non paion, nè rade,
  nè corruscar, nè figlia di Taumante,
  che di là cangia sovente contrade.

(He began as follows: "There is nothing
  which can affect the Mountain's holy way
  outside its order, or beyond its custom.
Here it is free from every kind of change;
  only what the heavens from themselves receive
  can work as cause here, nothing else avails:
for no rain ever, and no snow, no sleet,
  no dew, no frost, falls higher than the stairway

of the three little steps that are so brief.
Thick clouds do not appear, nor thin and misty,
 nor flash of lightning, nor Taumante's daughter,
 who there below often changes her country.)

The daughter of Thaumas (*Taumante* in Italian) is Iris, the rainbow. The whole passage is quiet, and it evokes the very feel of a mountain height; but at the same time it defines the mode of being of Statius, Virgil, and the Pilgrim, by means of the scene in which they meet. Below the three short steps leading to the gates of purgatory proper, lie the foothills of the *Antipurgatorio*, which is on earth as we know it, and subject to earth's weather. The spirits in that realm are saved by grace from Hell, but the scene in which they exist reveals no more of the way to spiritual growth than the world of nature does; hence the nostalgic "modern" lyricism we noticed in that realm. But beyond the gates, the scene, though still a mountain, itself points the way. We noticed that, during the second Day, everything the Pilgrim sees—the blank terrace of rock, the blaze of light as the sun sets, the cloud of anger— reveals the truth of his inner being at that moment. And the end of that sequence, in which love, in the effort of repentance, turns inward, is the soul's knowledge of itself. Now, on the third Day, the soul turns outward again; and now it can see the scene in which it finds itself in a new way. It is ready to understand what Statius explains about the Mountain scene: it is not the scene of earth as we know it below, but God's handiwork, the circling heavens unobscured; and everything in it points the upward way. The shaking of the Mountain, then, was not to be understood as an earthquake, but as a shudder of triumph and a sign with many meanings.

Statius proceeds to connect the significant scene of the Mountain and its tremor with the *moto spiritale* which carried him to this height (line 58):

Tremaci quando alcuna anima monda
sentesi, sì che surga, o che si mova
per salir su, e tal grido seconda.
Della mondizia sol voler fa prova,
che, tutta libera a mutar convento,
l'alma sorprende, e di voler le giova.

(It trembles when some spirit feels so cleansed
that she can arise, or can move to go
upward, and such a cry follows her then.
Of the cleansing, the will gives proof alone,
surprising the soul, all free to change her
cloister, availing her to will to go.)

Statius' formula for the moment of release and upward movement is worth mulling over. The will—by which he means
something more like "libido" (or *amor*) than our narrowly
rationalized "will"—changes its direction, moves upward.
Its new cleanliness, its freedom, and its movement are one,
or aspects of the same thing. The soul knows this experience, but not its final cause, which is above, in the direction
of its new movement. So the movement of the freed soul is
caused by Heaven, like the Mountain scene where the travellers meet.

With the end of Statius' explanation, which gives the
travellers a deeper recognition of themselves, each other, and
their marvellous situation, we are reminded again of the
Pilgrim and his thirst (line 73 ff.); and then Virgil starts
the next movement, asking Statius, with the greatest courtesy,
who he is.

In identifying himself (lines 82-102) Statius is obliged to
start with History—with the circumstances of time, and
place, and human society, in which all mortals have their
being. He was born under the Roman Empire, when Titus
destroyed Jerusalem, thus avenging the Crucifixion: another reference to the many connections between the In-

carnation and the summit of human reason and justice. The effect of this is to add another dimension to the scene, and to our understanding of the spirits who here "recognize" each other. This is the historic, or in medieval terms, the "allegorical" dimension: we begin to see that this moment, when Statius, Virgil, and the Pilgrim meet on their crossing paths, means (or is the meaning of) that great watershed of time and human history when the pagan ages ended and the age of Christianity began. Statius proceeds, having named himself, to specify that it was Virgil who gave him his being as a poet, when he got the clue (as Dante also had done) by reading the *Aeneid*.

This is the climax of the whole recognition scene, and the beginning of the peripeteia. The travellers, through their questioning of each other, have come to see who and where they are, first literally (high on the Mountain of purification, beyond the earthly weather); then morally, or tropologically (they are free to move upward); and finally allegorically. Their experience here is analogous to that of the ancient world when Revelation was already making its way among men. The Pilgrim, with his thirst, has been given much to drink, but not yet what the woman of Samaria asked for. And now, when Statius is on the very edge of recognizing Virgil with all that will mean to him as a mortal and a poet, the temptation (though felt as such) is irresistible to put too much love into the personal relations now dawning, as though they could finally slake the thirst of this realm.

The last act of recognition (lines 103-136) brings the peripeteia: i.e., the limitations of this high converse are perceived at the very moment when all is clear. The eager Pilgrim—the central intelligence, as James would have called him—takes the center of the stage. His smile, when Statius gives his tribute to Virgil, betrays to Statius that he knows something he is not saying. Virgil makes him a sign to be still; but when Statius presses, Virgil relents, and the Pilgrim has the pleasure of satisfying Statius, as he thinks at the moment. Statius also, for the moment, is moved, as though he saw what would truly slake his thirst (line 130):

Già si chinava ad abbracciar li piedi
al mio dottor; ma egli disse: "Frate,
non far, chè tu se'ombra, ed ombra vedi."
Ed ei surgendo: "Or puoi la quantitate
comprender dell'amor ch'a te mi scalda,
quando dismento nostra vanitate,
trattando l'ombre come cosa salda."

(Then he stooped down to clasp my teacher's feet,
but he said to him: "Brother, do not so,
for you are shadow, shadow what you see."
And he, as he arose: "Now you may know
how great the love that, toward you warming me,
makes me forget our emptiness, and so
treat as a solid thing the shadowy.")

The four lines which end the canto have been admired and quoted several times by Mr. T. S. Eliot. Certainly they have, even by themselves, the mysterious force of great poetry: they reach us intimately, and so prove, once more, that Dante's fiction of the world beyond the grave is a device for revealing, with unexpected depth and clarity, the human condition as we may sense it here. But it is characteristic of Dante that he controls the overtones of meaning which we associate with poetry, by means of the whole dramatic context. And the final recognition between Virgil, Statius, and the marvelling Pilgrim yields more pleasure and insight when one sees it as the end of the little play, the joyful triumph of vision and sympathy which is also tragic.

Virgil and Statius recover from their high greed (or avarice or over-generosity) almost at the moment of yielding to it. In terms of the dramatic form of the whole playlet, one might say that the peripeteia and final recognition are one. This light, rapid movement-of-spirit—a playing with

the sense of mortality—is characteristic of the third Day.
And the reader will notice how Dante's poetic or dramatic
style has been changed in order to give us this new experience. It is full of allusions, but the allusions are under-em-
phasized, and never explicitly explored. It is full of thought,
but there is no theorizing, no formal discursive development, no "philosophy." The thought and meaning is more
directly sensed: in the actions of the three travellers, in their
delicate responses to each other, in their swift sense of the
"Occasion" which brings them together and will soon lead
them apart.

Admirers of Henry James's late style—essentially dramatic, based upon the interplay of spirits who are extremely
"aware," and too fine for abstract concepts to violate them—
will, I think, find this part of the *Purgatorio* oddly Jamesian.
Dante was presenting the high point of pagan culture as he
understood it, the moment when it was not Christian but
full of premonitions of Christianity; and he was paying
tribute to the spirit of Virgil, to which he owed so much.
He could not have foreseen that later writers would, in due
time, explore analogous realms of experience, and find analogous dramatic styles to present them in. Racine's heroes,
for example, are hardly Christian in the medieval sense, but
rather pagans refined by the Christian hope they do not
share. They also have a preternatural sensitivity to personal
relations; they also never lose their urbanity; and when they
face their destiny as they really feel it, they unconsciously
echo the renunciations of Statius and Virgil which we have
just read:

> Adieu. Servons tous trois d'exemple à l'univers
> De l'amour la plus tendre et la plus malheureuse
> Dont il puisse garder l'histoire douloureuse.

I do not mean to imply, for a moment, that Jamesian or
Racinian echoes of this part of the *Purgatorio* reproduce
either Dante's style or his experience identically. Racine's

three lines above are enough to remind one of the high-style characteristic of his time. And James's syntactical complexities, whereby he struggles through the furniture of the British drawing-room to the ascetic clarity of his moral sense, do not sound like Dante either. Dante never loses his flexibility and modesty, his *sermo humilis*, or "humble speech," as Professor Auerbach has pointed out—even when he shows a high point of humane heroism and urbanity. Perhaps that extraordinary work, *La Princesse de Clèves*, is closer to the style and spirit of this scene, for there the effort of the enlightened human to satisfy its love in accord with reason and virtue is seen as both comic and tragic. None of these parallels is exact. But they help one understand the Pilgrim's swift life in this realm.

As for the travellers who see their own ghostliness, they recover at once, continuing their conversation and their journey. In order to follow them with understanding, it is necessary to pause, and to turn from the course of the poem to the work of Dante the author as he arranges the scenes and the episodes of the literal narrative. The next two chapters are devoted to the symbolism of the characters and the verse.

🎝 CHAPTER 15. THE NEW
LIFE OF HISTORY

How CAN IT BE that Virgil and Statius, dead more than a thousand years, can speak and move and answer questions? How can the Pilgrim, nourished in another time, culture and language, hear and see them? How (for that matter) can we be moved by these scenes six hundred years after Dante wrote them?

Such questions as these hover in the background of Canto XXII, as the travellers continue their climb after their touching recognition of each other, talking of poetry and of the spirits they have admired, and skirting the mystery of their present communion. It is true that from the beginning of the *Commedia*, when Virgil first appeared, the spirits of the dead have been visible and audible. And from time to time the anomalies of this ghostly life have puzzled the Pilgrim. In the *Antipurgatorio*, for example, he found to his dismay that he could not embrace the spirit of his friend Casella. And he was troubled by the fact that he alone cast a shadow. But now he is nearing the end of the journey which he was then beginning; his insight has deepened through experience; he is beginning to see almost as much as the author himself sees about this strange realm of being. And Canto XXII is full of hints to the Pilgrim, and even more to the reader, about the nature of Virgil's and Statius's life here on the Mountain of purification.

The reader, perhaps, has accepted the spirits of the dead without question, as make-believe only, part of the basis of the whole fiction. After all, we are used to fictive or dramatic evocations of the past, from Shakespeare down to the latest historical novel. We have no difficulty in accepting such fictions because we attribute little significance or validity to them; and it never occurs to us to demand their credentials. But Dante meant Virgil and Statius as seriously as a writer can mean anything. He took full responsibility for them, and when he built them into the very foundations of his poem, he knew, in many ways, just what he was doing. Professor Curtius has spoken of "an ideal realm" in Dante's Christian epic, "in which all the great figures of the West are gathered: the Emperors (Augustus, Trajan, Justinian); the Church Fathers; the Teachers of the seven Liberal Arts; the Lights of Philosophy; the Founders of religious orders, the mystics." When Dante writes at the beginning of the *Purgatorio*, "ma qui la morta poesì risurga" ("here may dead poetry rise again"), he might have added an invocation of History also, for he intended his poem to present the truth of history.

I observed (in Chapter 12) that when Dante wrote the *Commedia* he no longer believed that the life and meaning of the past could be grasped by means of purely rational principles. He did not see the great figures of history as illustrations of his own moral principles, as he had tried to do in the *Convivio*, with its rationalistic "allegory of poets," but as concrete, many-sided human individuals with their roles in the drama of history which Christian faith reveals, a drama in which he too had a role. In his poetry he turned from the allegory of poets to the allegory of theologians, which he explains in his *Letter to Can Grande*. If one is to understand the poetry of the third Day, in which the Christian understanding of history begins to emerge, one needs to know a little about the traditional allegory of theologians which Dante here uses for his own purposes.

Professor Auerbach's monograph, *Figura*, is a study of the development of this allegory by the Fathers of the Church. They developed it as a means of understanding, or "interpreting" Scripture. By that means they understood the history of the ancient Hebrews as a sign, or "figure," of Christ's coming; they believed that the meaning of Old Testament history was not clear until its "fulfillment" in Christ. The great value of Professor Auerbach's study is that he applies his erudition directly to Dante's poem and Dante's methods of composition. The Virgil whom we meet in the *Commedia* "is indeed the human Virgil," he writes, "but not only that; for the historic is only a figure of the fulfilled truth, which the poem reveals, and this 'fulfillment' is more, is more real, is more significant, than the figure." Dante intends Virgil in his poem to be more significant than the historic Virgil in his ancient Rome, because of the wider context—that of Christian understanding—in which he places him.

Professor Auerbach shows that the method of "Figural Interpretation," as he calls it, had pagan as well as Christian sources, for late pagan writers also tried to make their history and past literature significant and living again in their generation. But he finds the prototype of the method in Saint Paul's interpretation of the Old Testament (page 43). The sufferings of the Jews, Saint Paul says (I Corinthians 10.6), are to be understood as a figure (*figura*) of the sufferings of Christians in their difficult time: that is, the Jews, real people, really suffered at a certain moment of time in a real wilderness; but the meaning (or "fulfillment," as Professor Auerbach calls it) of that historic episode is the suffering of Christians in the light of Revelation. The Christians' suffering is also real in its historic time and place. It is therefore not identical with the wilderness ordeal recorded in the Old Testament—real historic events are never identical with each other—but it is analogous to it. The meaning of the first event is to be found in the second, which, lighted by Revelation, is its "fulfillment." The distinguishing mark of *figura* as a technique for grasping the life and meaning of past historic persons and events, is that both the past event and the later event which is its meaning—both figure and fulfillment—are real, concrete, and historic.

It is difficult for us, with our conceptualizing habits of mind, to accept or even to understand the method of *figura*, which derives a sort of direct, non-conceptual "light" from the analogical relationship of two events widely separated in time. But Professor Auerbach shows that this method of interpretation was a major instrument whereby the Church Fathers, in a confused and cosmopolitan time like ours, preserved the achievements of Hebrew and Greek, and in due time transmitted them to Dante's Europe. What they transmitted was not merely Hebrew Law or Greek Philosophy, but the sense of the reality *and* meaning of the historic life of the ancient peoples, a life different from that of subsequent times, but significant still. "The great majority of the allegories one encounters," Professor Auerbach writes, page 48, "present something like a virtue (e.g., Wisdom) or a passion (e.g., Jealousy) or an institution (Law); perhaps the most general synthesis of a historic phenomenon (Peace, the Fatherland): never the full historic reality of a definite event." That is the kind of abstract, or neoplatonizing, or pagan-literary allegory which Dante called the "allegory of poets," and gave up as inadequate when he abandoned the *Convivio*. By the time he came to write the *Commedia* he had decided to use the lore of *figura* for his own purposes. He must have felt that it offered the one means of making his art "living-within-history" (*innergeschichtlich*), as Professor Auerbach says of *figura*: "a new beginning and a new birth of the formative (*gestaltenden*) powers."

Thus the historic Virgil lives again in Dante's poem; a past life is reaffirmed in a later age and in a wider perspective which "fulfills it": i.e., gives it its full meaning. But the uniqueness of this past life, all the circumstances of time and place and individual character which make it different from the present, is not thereby denied. On the contrary: the irreversible pastness of the past is an essential part of its present meaning.

There is a beautiful instance of the way this works for Virgil in Canto xxii, in the famous tribute which the Christianized Statius pays to him (line 64):

Ed egli a lui: "Tu prima m'inviasti
    verso Parnaso a ber nelle sue grotte,
    e poi appresso Dio m'alluminasti.
Facesti come quei che va di notte,
    che porta il lume retro e sè non giova,
    ma dopo sè fa le persone dotte,
quando dicesti: 'Secol si rinnova;
    torna giustizia e primo tempo umano,
    e progenie discende dal ciel nuova.' "

(He said to him: "You were the first who sent me
    on to Parnassus' grottoes, to imbibe,
    then on the way toward God your light you lent me.
You did as one who, going through the night,
    bears light at his back, and does not profit thence
    but makes those wise who follow on behind,
When you said, 'The world is renewed again;
    justice returns, and the first human time,
    from Heaven a new progeny descends.' ")

The lines quoted by Statius are from Virgil's Fourth Eclogue, which the Middle Ages regarded as an inspired prophecy of Christianity. There is no doubt that their spirit *is* pre-Christian, perhaps like Messianic utterances in the Old Testament. But in Statius' tribute Virgil is not Christianized, nor falsified or distorted in any other way. On the contrary, his paganism is the more deep, consistent, and touching for being presented in the new scene, the Christian *saeculum*, which he never saw. "Some one said: 'The dead writers are remote from us because we *know* so much more than they do.' Precisely, and they are that which we know." This remark of T. S. Eliot's (in *Tradition and the Individual Talent*) is intended to reveal the relationships within a living tradition; it applies very exactly to Dante's relation to Virgil.

But the Virgil we meet here is, in spite of his vitality and many-sided humanity, a character in Dante's poem. Can we say, then, that he is to be regarded as the fulfillment of the historic Virgil in the same way in which Saint Paul's Christians were regarded as the fulfillment of the Hebrews in the Wilderness?

The answer to this question must, I think, be no, not in the same way. Dante regarded his poem as fictive, and even insisted upon his work as poet, or maker of the fiction. He could hardly have believed in the literal reality of his fictive scenes and characters, as Saint Paul believed in the historic fulfillment of the historic sufferings of the Jews. Moreover, he often mentions the literary sources of his fiction. In *Inferno*, Canto xxv, lines 94-99, for example, he boasts with grim irony that he is outdoing Lucan and Ovid. In *Purgatorio*, Canto xxix, line 100 ff., he cites Ezekiel and John as authorities for the vision he is then describing. In his *Letter to Can Grande,* beginning at section 20 (Temple Classics edition) he adduces authorities both pagan and Christian for every element in the Prologue to the *Paradiso*. And when he first meets Virgil himself, in the dark wood, and craves his living guidance, he relies upon his study of Virgil's book (*Inferno*, Canto i, line 82):

> "vagliame il lungo studio e il grande amore,
> che m'ha fatto cercar lo tuo volume."

> ("May the long study avail me, and the great
> love, which has led me to search your volume.")

It is of the essence of Dante's sturdy realism as well as of his literary culture, which Professor Curtius has shown us, that he should rely on the texts he knew, and acknowledge them in an almost "scholarly" manner, just as he acknowledged his poetic labors. But he takes responsibility for the truthfulness of his poetic labors also. He believed that the imaginative act of spirit whereby he grasped a historic or legendary life and then imitated it in his drama and his verse, could also give truth, provided it was moved by a sufficiently enlightened love.

The masters of *figura* had seen, since Tertullian, Professor Auerbach tells us, that this historiographic method depends upon an act of spirit—a direct, sympathetic effort of understanding—whereby the figure and its fulfillment are grasped together, their meanings revealed in each other's light. Both the figure and the fulfillment are individual, concrete, incarnate; "only the understanding, the *intellectus spiritualis*," he writes (page 47), "is an act of spirit, which must comprehend each of the two poles with the given or hoped-for materials of the past, present, or future event." Dante's act-of-spirit comprehends the historic Virgil in his writings and what he knew of the facts of his life, and the fulfilled Virgil in the innumerable contexts of the fictive journey. The realms of the *Inferno* and the *Purgatorio* are not real as God's world is real; the Virgil who appears there is not real as the Christians of Saint Paul's time were real. But the act-of-spirit whereby Dante grasps the historic Virgil and the Virgil of the *Commedia* is truthful, he believes, in the same way as Saint Paul's historic understanding was true. In both cases the understanding is formed and authenticated by the love of Christ. Christ, appearing at a moment in history, gives forms and meaning to the temporal sequence itself. At the same time the love of Christ (available to humanity since the Incarnation) can form the life (or actions) of the human spirit in accord with truth. Insofar as Dante or Saint Paul was moved, in the effort to understand history, by the love of Christ, this effort of understanding gave truth.

In Cantos XXI and XXII, such a loving act of understanding, which both affirms the irreversible movement of history and transcends it, is figured and dramatized in the relationships between Dante the Pilgrim, Virgil, and Statius, who never knew each other in the flesh. They knew only each other's writings—signs or outward appearances of the spirit's life in time. By a creative or poetic act of love they go through the sign to the life behind it, as Virgil says (Canto xxii, line 10):

> "Amore,
> acceso di virtù, sempre altro accese,
> pur che la fiamma sua paresse fuore."

> ("Love, kindled by virtue, kindles another always, if its flame but appear without.")

Virgil puts it in his humane terms, as reason may recognize it. We see that he and Statius and the Pilgrim make mistakes. Virgil, for instance, thinks Statius must have been avaricious on earth when as a matter of fact he was a spendthrift. Statius, when he first recognized Virgil, forgot the distinction between that visionary being and the full reality of a fleshly mortal man. With their humane understanding they do not know what Dante the author knows about this realm. Dante the author understands their shadowy beings as dependent upon Christ, and their appearance here as signs, or figures, of the risen Christ.

The fictive scenes of the third Day do not exactly represent the love-inspired work of Dante the author, but they are very close to it, and the higher we climb the closer does the Pilgrim's understanding come to the author's. In his dream of the Siren, his loving study made her move and speak; but the love was only the amoral appetite of the flesh. When he meets Virgil and Statius, he sees those poets recognize each other across the gap of time; but the love is only that—in their understanding of it—which any and all virtuous spirits have for each other: timeless, and without definite historic meaning. But when Statius places Virgil at that great watershed of history, with pagan civilization one way and Christian the other, we are very close to the love which enabled Dante the author, meeting Virgil hoarse with long silence, to bring him alive and to make him move and speak again in the new time. For the fictive spirits of the past in the poem—the remote past, and the dead of Dante's own time—are fulfillments (in Professor Auerbach's illuminating terms) of real, individual fleshly people, each with his significant place in the significant temporal sequence of history. Both history itself and Dante's visionary fulfillment of it are figures of Christ; in Dante's belief, Christ was the clue both to the life and meaning of history, and to the life and meaning of his poem-making.

Dante's understanding of history looks queer, remote, and limited to us. We know vastly more than he did, not only about his Mediterranean civilization, but about civilizations in other parts of the world which he never dreamed of; and we know that in the last six hundred years vast changes have come to man and his notions of the world. We lack his faith—for I suppose that even professing Christians cannot believe as he did. But we can see, I think, that he sought to understand history in the only possible way: by analogy with what he knew and believed in his own time and place. He did not neglect facts; on the contrary, he had the greatest respect for them, and collected all the facts then available. But he knew, like all our competent contemporary historians, that facts alone have neither form nor meaning. To make history an act of the spirit is required; and for that creative act of sympathy and understanding—of love, in his terms—he took more responsibility than other historians accept. The *Commedia* shows not only his view of history, but the severe discipline whereby he formed his spirit into an agent capable of apprehending history.

At the point we have reached in the purgatorial journey we are almost ready for Dante's description of his own poetry, the famous formula for the *dolce stil nuovo* in Canto xxiv. When we reach that point I shall have a few more observations to make on Dante's severe conception of his art. Meanwhile, Dante the Pilgrim must explore the realm of timeless humanism a little further, before the reality of history, where the poem is being composed, shows through the vision of the Mountain and its denizens.

ᕗ CHAPTER 16. THE FRAGRANT TREES: PARADOXES OF HUMAN NOURISHMENT

AT THE END of Canto XXII (line 134 ff.) the walking and pleasant talking of Virgil, Statius, and the Pilgrim are interrupted when they suddenly come to a tree in the middle of their path. The tree rises without branches so high as to prevent its climbing, and grows bigger at the top. It is loaded with fragrant fruit, and freshened by a clear spring which sprays over it from the rock above. A voice is heard crying, "Of this food you shall have dearth." And then it recites examples of abstinence: Mary's selfless thought for the marriage-feast, the asceticism of the ancient Romans, Daniel's meagre diet, and John the Baptist's honey and locusts. All of the examples are associated with the delights of natural felicity, both "the first human time," the classical myth of the Golden Age, and, by way of Mary and John the Baptist, the Christian notion of nature redeemed.

The appearance of this tree, breaking into the conversation, is at first arbitrary and surprising, like most of the changes of focus in the purgatorial journey. It is also paradoxical in its immediate effect, for its delectable fruits are both good, with their Eden-like associations, and unattainable. But it does not take long for the travellers (or the attentive reader) to get its immediate dramatic *raison d'être*. It marks the entrance into the terrace where gluttony is repented, and, as usual, suggests the cure for that sin in advance, so that when we meet it more intimately it will be seen truly, and suffered, not for itself, but for a good end. Because the Pilgrim's spirit is so free, alert, and forewarned at this height, he senses the whole sequence of repentance at once, in the paradoxical impressions of the tree itself.

The tree also resumes, in another way, the theme of the Pilgrim's natural-supernatural thirst, which burns through the more and more intense visions of the whole third Day; and, in this aspect, the tree is more significant still. In fact, it is an important symbol in the poem, from its first appearance here, to the end in the *Paradiso Terrestre*. What, then, does it mean?

It is of course a traditional symbol derived from the "allegory of theologians" which Dante inherited, and which I briefly discussed in the last chapter. It is based (in part) on the trees in Genesis, the Tree of the Knowledge of Good and Evil, Chapter 2, and the Tree of Life, Chapter 3. When the travellers leave the terrace of gluttony they will pass another tree like this first one, and learn that it was raised from the tree Eve tasted, the Tree of Knowledge, therefore. The theme of the tree's forbidden fruits recurs in many ways above, and the tree, or trees, themselves reappear in many very complex contexts in *Paradiso Terrestre*, where they are associated with the Cross of Christ as their truth or fulfillment. There is, I think, an echo, though faint and transmuted, of their nourishment even in *Paradiso*, Canto II, where the "bread of angels" is mentioned. Thus it is evident that Dante wishes at least to *suggest* many meanings in the tree-symbol, and for this reason it has set many generations of commentators to disputing. Is the first tree the Tree of Life, as the second is certainly the Tree of Knowledge or are they both from the Tree of Knowledge? Or does Dante wish to indicate a mysterious identity (beyond human capacity to grasp, perhaps) between Life and Knowledge? When one tries to understand the trees here and in *Paradiso Terrestre*, any sort of univocal interpretation becomes nearly impossible.

I do not propose to attempt such an interpretation of these trees, but to examine their role in the drama at this point, i.e., the use Dante makes of this symbol to foreshadow the next phase in the Pilgrim's growth. The tree-symbol, like the figures of Virgil and Statius which we discussed in the last chapter, are derived from Christian methods of interpretation, and Dante uses both to show the Pilgrim's growing understanding of history in Christian terms. The whole third Day shows how, to the general moral-psychological grasp of human life and growth, the "trope" in medieval terms, is added the more concrete knowledge of the Pilgrim's actual place in history, the "allegory" as this level of meaning was called—*Allegoria, quid credas*: "The allegory, what you must believe." The trees signify both man's original disobedience, Eve's sampling of the apple, and his Redemption, Christ's suffering on the Cross. That is what the Christian must believe. And this belief, fixing the crucial dates in the history of the race, will enable the Pilgrim to place his own historic moment, and to feel both its promise and its frightening responsibilities.

But what the travellers immediately see before them is a real tree, complete with trunk and branches, leaves and fruits; and, like any tree, it speaks first to their famished senses.

The delicious odor of the tree's unattainable fruit makes everything savory, even acorns or locusts. But in Canto XXIII, as the travellers meet the repentant gluttonous, they see these properties of the tree reflected in unexpected ways in the visible shapes of the human creature: images of starvation (line 31):

> Parean l'occhiaie anella senza gemme:
> chi nel viso degli uommi legge *omo*,
> ben avria quivi conosciuto l'*emme*.

> (The eye-sockets looked like rings with no gem:
> he who in the human face reads *omo*,
> would easily have recognized the *M*.)

Dante is thinking of the bones of the face as letters, O M O, *homo*: ꧁ꙩꙩ꧂. It is perhaps the most striking of a number of images of the fluctuations of the flesh in response to the hunger and thirst of the spirit which the tree and its fruits produce. So the travellers can grasp the spiritual root of gluttony, and so the reader may see the analogy between the greeds for poetry, philosophy, and the other fruits of the human spirit which have impeded Virgil, Statius, and the Pilgrim in their climb, and the literal greed for food and drink which is here repented. In both cases—both material and intellectual food—the true satisfaction is represented by the unattainable fruits of the tree. And the result of mistaking the shadow for the Reality is seen in the famished face of "homo," as it was, in Canto XXI, in the insubstantial shadowiness of Virgil and Statius.

The general notion that the shape of the human body—its obesity or emaciation, its rosiness or pallor, its flabbiness or its muscle-tone—may have psychological causes and accurately reflect the psyche's postures and focuses, is familiar enough in modern medicine. Not only does the body influence the mind, the mind also affects the body; the psychosomatic relationship goes both ways. And Cannon coined the suggestive phrase "the body thinks." It is because Dante knew this so well that he could make the life of the spirit sensuously present in bodily imagery of every description, touching our most intimate (and usually censored) feeling for human life. He shows us that Virgil knows all this also. He knows that the Pilgrim would waste his time (and his being) if he paused too long to dote upon the unattainable fruits. Virgil has his own true lore of the life of the soul in the body, and his own ascetic ethic. He could interpret gluttony and its cure in his own pagan, moral-psychological terms; and though he does not know how the Pilgrim's hunger and thirst could be satisfied, he knows that the goods of earth (the fruits of trees or of human philosophy) are inadequate. His sad wisdom suffices to show the moral interpretation of the mysterious tree, and to warn the Pilgrim away from its delights (line 4).

It is left to the spirit of Forese Donati to suggest the Christian meaning of the tree, its "allegoria," or specific historic significance. Forese was a close friend of Dante's during the time when Dante was absorbed in pagan philosophy, and also (as many students of his biography now agree) in the pleasures of the senses, which his love-poems, and his bawdy and humorous exchanges with Forese, clearly record. When he meets Forese here, we see him after he has received the grace to repent; and he now sees his life, and Dante's, in a Christian light. Both his remorse and his new hope are outside Virgil's philosophy; and so his explanation of the tree adds another dimension to Virgil's understanding (line 67):

> "Di bere e di mangiar n'accende cura
> l'odor ch'esce del pomo, e dello sprazzo
> che si distende su per la verdura.
> E non pure una volta, questo spazzo
> girando, si rinfresca nostra pena,
> io dico pena e dovrei dir sollazzo;
> chè quella voglia all'arbore ci mena,
> che menò Cristo lieto a dire: 'Elì,'
> quando ne liberò con la sua vena."

> ("A need is lit in us to drink and eat
> by the scent of the apples, and the spray
> which from above spreads over all the green.
> And not once only, on this circling way,
> is the pain refreshed within us newly,
> and yet not pain but solace I should say:
> for that desire leads us to the tree
> which led Christ in his joy to say: 'Eli,'
> when with his opened veins he made us free.")

Virgil had accepted the tree as a natural tree only, and the thirst it wakened in the same way, without enquiring into meanings or causes behind nature. Forese starts his account of the tree in naturalistic terms which Virgil could follow, but goes on to point out the analogy between his passion of purgation, his repeatedly-thwarted desire to eat and drink, his dying-to-live, and the sacrificial act of Christ on the Cross. In this context the tree is seen as not only a tree—*any* tree in nature—but a sign of the most significant Tree of all.

Professor Auerbach points out (in his *Figura*) that these trees are very ancient symbols which, like the figures which we looked at in the last chapter, Dante inherited from the long tradition of the "allegory of theologians." Professor Auerbach proceeds to distinguish such symbols from *figura*. The figure—the Hebrews in the wilderness, for example— is essentially and from the beginning historic, and a bearer of meaning in the whole historic sequence. But the symbol does not necessarily refer to history at all. Its effect is natural and immediate; and its meaning is an interpretation of nature, and of human life, in general and in nature. What it symbolizes is always something of great importance, even holy; and the symbol itself has power. Often magic force is ascribed to it. All of this applies to the tree, as the travellers first meet it: it symbolizes human nourishment, and has a "magical" power over those who approach it. Professor Auerbach goes on to explain that a natural symbol of this kind may be given, in addition a historic meaning; and that too applies to these trees. Such trees no doubt had an ancient symbolic value even at the time when Genesis was written, and similar symbolic trees occur in many peoples' art and literature, quite outside the western tradition. But the Hebrew and then the Christian tradition took over that natural symbol and without "denaturing" it, incorporated it into the vast system centering in historic Revelation. Professor Auerbach writes that the Eucharist, in which the mysteries of human nourishment are contained, is the classic instance of a symbol of this kind, "natural" or "cosmic" in the sacred feasts of primitive peoples, "historic" as transformed by Christianity.

Father Daniélou's account of the development of Christian symbolism agrees with the sequence noted by Professor Auerbach, but puts it, of course, in Christian terms: "The revelation of God, as it is made known to us by Scripture, is a progressive revelation," he writes, "for God is made known first in his manifestation through the cosmos. Thereafter He reveals Himself through His successive interventions in history. But each of these revelations, though it transcends the preceding, does not destroy it, but continues and assumes it. Thus the cosmic symbols by which God is known in natural religion are adopted by the Abrahamic and Christic religions, but they are changed into a new sense. For now the waters of Baptism are charged not only with the content of the Cosmic Deluge, but also with that of the Mosaic exodus across the Red Sea and the descent of Christ into the waters of death. The vernal Easter feast now commemorates not only the first creation in spring-time, but also the re-creation of the people of God at the time of the exodus and the creation of the new universe through the resurrection of Christ."

Did Dante wish to suggest the Eucharist also, by means of these trees, and so add to their mythic, historic, and doc-trinal references a ritual element also? I do not know. But it is certain that they symbolize, both in their natural and in their historic aspects, the paradoxes of human nourish-ment: nourishment for the flesh and for the spirit; delight and renunciation, feast and sacrifice in one.

It is certain also that the Pilgrim's sense of the meanings of the trees grows and deepens in the same way as the tra-ditional interpretation grew. The Pilgrim sees the tree first literally as a natural tree; he sees and smells it. Then he understands it as a symbol of human nourishment, physical and spiritual. And finally he sees it (though briefly, in Forese's reference) as the *super*natural object of faith, in which the human effort to satisfy the spirit's hunger and thirst finds its mysterious goal: the Cross of Christ. That is the sequence which Professor Auerbach and Father Daniélou have sketched as the history of the development of Christian symbolism out of primitive and pagan sources. Dante of course did not have the benefit of modern researches into comparative religion and the totems and rituals of primitive peoples. But he had an uncanny insight into the psychology of his own individual history, and of the process whereby he accepted the Christian faith as the completion and reinterpretation of his Virgilian literary and philosophic culture. And at this point in the Pilgrim's journey, we begin to see that the chief phases of the history of the human spirit, as Dante understood them, are reflected in the mutations of the Pilgrim's inner life.

The appearance of the tree broke through the communion of Virgil and Statius at the high point of human awareness where classical culture senses the new age coming on. The effect of this break-through upon the Pilgrim is (as we shall see below) both sobering and frightening. It is all very well to contemplate the course of history as we did in Cantos xxi and xxii, in the cool light of "timeless humanism," in the quiet atmosphere of the Mountain height above all earthly weather, and in the beautiful image of Virgil's light passing through the pagan darkness. But the tree speaks directly in terms of human thirst, and stimulates the most intimate awareness of mortal life, where the insatiate spirit turns this way and that in its fattening and thinning, swelling and withering fleshly sheath. The sense of history, of the burden and significance of the concrete, individual human creature in his time and place, will inspire the Pilgrim, yet at the same time frighten him, like an actor who suddenly sees that the curtain is up, all eyes on him, and the play more serious and immediate than he had thought.

〰 CHAPTER 17. CANTO XXV:
THE PERILOUS PASSAGE

CANTO XXV records the travellers' climb from the terrace of the repentant gluttonous, with its beautiful and tantalizing trees, to the terrace where the lustful are refined in the flame. As the travellers hurry upward, the Pilgrim mulls over his experiences below, and tries to prepare for ordeals ahead, as he does in all of the transitions from one terrace to the next above. But the transition and stock-taking of Canto XXV is particularly important, for it is the last time the Pilgrim can reflect upon his movement-of-spirit during the third Day. He will be too occupied with the testimony of the spirits he meets in the flame for any reflections, and when he leaves that terrace his own ordeal (crossing the wall of fire guarding Eden) will be almost upon him, and the night which will close the third Day will be already approaching.

I pointed out in the last chapter that one of the effects of the fragrant trees, with their paradoxical appeal to the deepest human appetites, was to give the Pilgrim a sharper and more searching sense of his own individual destiny, with its frightening promise and responsibility. From that point onward the Pilgrim himself gradually comes into focus, no longer as the mere reflector of the action, the Jamesian spectator, but as the protagonist of the drama. At the same time, and by the same token, Dante the Pilgrim and Dante the author are gradually revealed as one. The point at which they coincide, the climax of this sequence (and of so much else) when Dante's own name is mentioned for the first and only time, is the meeting with Beatrice, in Canto xxx, line 55.

In Canto XXV the Pilgrim merely begins to realize and prepare for his own crucial action and passion. In Canto XXII, after the touching recognition between Statius and

Virgil, he had heard the sages talking over that mystery and agreeing that it was made possible by an outward manifestation of love. Now he thinks over the fragrant trees, and the spirits whose repentant passion made them return to the trees again and again in their circling. These meditations suggest the spirit's power over the flesh, and the alarming possibility of an act of spirit not determined by the flesh. The Pilgrim's action in this canto is presented in two chief themes, that of the climb itself, up a narrow way and along a dangerous ledge, and that of his attempts, with Virgil's and then Statius' aid to understand that power of spirit which he saw in the wasted faces of the repentant gluttonous. This action is deeper than either the physical climbing or Virgil's and Statius' explanations: it is an act of love or will, and of preconceptual awareness; and to present it Dante resumes many of the sensuous metaphors of the whole third Day.

The first tercet of the canto reminds us, by giving the position of the stars, that it is late—afternoon already; and the second tercet shows us the travellers hurrying under "the spur of need." The path, so narrow that they have to go in single file, ascends steeply (line 7):

> così entrammo noi per la callaia,
> uno innanzi altro, prendendo la scala
> che per artezza i salitor dispaia.
> E quale il cicognin che leva l'ala
> per voglia di volare, e non s'attenta
> d'abbandonar lo nido, e giù la cala:
> tal era io con voglia accesa e spenta
> di domandar, venendo infino all'atto
> che fa colui ch'a dicer s'argomenta.

> (So we entered through a gap in the rock,
> one before the other, there to begin
> the stair whose straitness makes the climbers part.

And like the little stork who lifts his wing
  with the desire to fly, and still does not
  try to forsake the nest, and lets it sink,
was I: my desire fired and put out
  to ask a question, even to the movement
  of one who prepares to speak in his own thought.)

Each traveller must make the climb on his own. Our attention is directed to the Pilgrim as he makes that effort,
like a young stork wishing to fly and not daring to. This
metaphor echoes kinesthetic images of flight and the preparation for flight in Canto xix, when the Pilgrim first senses
the action of the third Day. Now it serves to connect the
theme of physical ascent with an effort of understanding;
and this effort is also one of trust or faith, for the stork was
in the Middle Ages a traditional symbol of obedience.

In the next section (lines 16-30) Virgil tries to help the
Pilgrim with his question, how can the spirits of the repentant gluttonous whom he saw below grow lean, when
they must have no need of nourishment? Virgil does not
answer directly, but offers two illustrations of the connection between the spirit, in its need, and its sensuously-perceptible images: Meleager, whose life was consumed in the
burning brand, and the visible image of ourselves which
we may see flitting in a mirror. He also compares the Pilgrim's action as he asks the question with an arrow drawn
back to the tip and ready to fly; and at the end of the passage he suggests that the Pilgrim's spirit has a wound (the
wound of doubt), which Statius is the one to heal.

It is a bewildering wealth of imagery, reflecting much
that we have seen in the day's climb, and also the rapidity
of perception at this height. But the images are not imaginatively fused into one. They are more like witty associations, or the play of Coleridge's Fancy, or the merely illustrative "allegory of poets," than elements in an organic,
poetic whole. Virgil seems to know this himself; and he

uses his metaphors merely to open up the problem and to point quickly ahead to Statius and his answer.

The relation between the Pilgrim and Virgil at this moment echoes that moment in Canto xviii when Virgil saw, through the Pilgrim's eager, timid face, his spirit's need to question further, and answered with his discourse on "love in the human clay." But that was the farthest limit of Virgil's light: the soul as reason sees it, "the form of the body." Now the Pilgrim needs to understand how the soul, in its fluctuating life, may be perceptible without body; not only in the emaciation of the repentant gluttonous, but in this whole ghostly realm. This is a matter not of Eros, but of Agape, not of reason only, but of faith; hence a question for the Christian Statius to answer.

Statius' discourse occupies most of the canto, lines 34-108. He does what he can to make the mystery acceptable to that enlightened intellect which characterizes Virgil, the Pilgrim, and himself at this point. He sums up the Aristotelian notion of embryology, according to which the human foetus passes through plant-like, and then animal forms on its way to the human. This part of his discourse echoes Virgil's analogies (in Canto xviii) between physical movement, the life of growing plants, sentient animal life, and the human *moto spiritale*. It is (in spite of its outmoded terminology) not unlike modern notions of the development of the embryo and the evolution of the species. But when Statius comes to the change from animal to human he adds his Christian doctrine: he attributes that mutation to the direct intervention of God in the work of nature. God is the immediate cause of that potentiality of freedom and self-awareness which distinguishes the human from the animal soul, and God is also its final cause: the hidden goal of its love-moved life. So Virgil's picture of the psyche is extended before and after: to his image of the soul in nature and in its own reason's light, is added the beginning and ending which faith demands.

Statius picks his way very carefully through the philosophical and theological issues of Dante's time. It is one of the best places in which to study Dante's own doctrines, not only of the soul's life, but of poetry; for the philosophic issues are reflected in the varied practice of the poets of Dante's own school, that of the *dolce stil*. But what concerns us here is the effect which Statius' elucidations have upon Dante the Pilgrim, at this perilous moment in his upward struggle.

Statius (in contrast to Virgil) emphasizes the uniqueness of each human soul in two chief ways: each soul is created by a special act of God, and each soul has its mortal existence in its own unique body, hence its own destiny in a temporal context of its own. This is the theoretical basis of Dante the author's sharp realism, his sense of the meaning and reality of the tiniest and humblest acts of any human soul. It is, therefore, the basis of his "allegory of theologians," which stresses the meaning of history—that of the race and that of the individual—in contrast to Virgil's timeless (unhistoric) wisdom. As for Dante the Pilgrim, Statius' words confirm the nature of the ascent as he had felt it in the climb itself: he alone, at this point, must make an effort. His companions may encourage him, help, in a way, by example; but fundamentally the movement required here must be that of his own spirit.

At the end of his discourse Statius returns to the Pilgrim's immediate question, how the bodiless spirits of the repentant gluttonous may visibly waste away. If the human soul is breathed directly by God into the natural body, it has some sort of existence independent of the body. Death dissolves the body, but the bodiless soul is still both human and divine. It has memory, will (or love), and intellect, and also that "formative power" which made it the form of the body. Here beyond the grave it forms an aerial body, or shadow, which reveals the love that moves it. This love is not only God-given, but human, and formed thus partly by the habits acquired in mortal and fleshly life. And just as we recognize human spirits on earth by the sensuously-perceptible body they form and move, so here we see the spirit in its shadow. From this notion it is only a short step to the formative power ("virtu formativa") which makes the body of the *poem* we are reading: a shadow of the spirits of the dead made, not of air, but of language, by the poetic act obedient to Love. This is another indication of the fact that, as we approach the end of the purgatorial journey, the space between Pilgrim and author grows thinner and thinner.

It is obvious that Statius' words, though they in a way account for the experiences that wounded the Pilgrim with doubt, still require an act of faith if they are to be efficacious. And Dante the author certainly did not suppose that he had made the extra-corporeal existence and power of the human spirit—immortality in various analogues and aspects—acceptable to reason alone. When he tackled this problem in the *Convivio* (Fourth Treatise, Chapter xxi) he remarked, with his usual candor, "Let no man marvel if I speak in such wise as seems hard to understand; for to me myself it seems a marvel how such a producing [God's producing the separable soul in the body] can be arrived at by argument and perceived by the intellect; and it is not a thing to expound in language." Here in Canto xxv he presents Statius' discourse as the description of a marvel, and he shows the Pilgrim receiving it, not by reason, but by an act of faith affirming the spirit's power beyond reason, and beyond the human nature which reason can see. Virgil's picture in Canto xviii delighted the mind, for the moment, with its clarity and beauty. Statius' discourse is, on the contrary, not to be doted on; it frightens and tenses the Pilgrim by the daring affirmation of his own spirit's power which it seems to require. The Pilgrim had looked at the human soul in Virgil's light as it were disinterestedly, to enjoy the timeless truth and beauty of the vision. But here, where he takes his last quick look at his own soul he does so for extrinsic and practical reasons: like a man on the edge of a cliff who glances briefly at his feet, feeling the tension in his muscles, to estimate his strength for a dangerous leap.

The travellers reach the terrace where lust is purged in flame, just as Statius ends his discourse. This is the point where it is most necessary to affirm the spirit's power over the flesh, even beyond reason and nature. We saw lust as the easy, warm, and natural entrance to Hell; here it appears on the very edge of Eden, as the last peril of that very freedom of spirit which has been so hardly achieved. The moment Statius is silent the travellers turn without comment (line 111) to "another care," which is only another sign of the crisis of the spirit's life which underlies the whole canto: they turn to the perilous passage along the narrow ledge between the flame one way and the abyss the other.

The final sequence (lines 112-139) presents this passage, echoing many of the metaphors of the opening sequence of the canto. Here too the travellers must go in single file, each responsible for his own safety. The abyss along one side of the path, defended by no parapet, reminds us of the feelings of the young stork trying to make up his mind to risk himself in the air. Virgil's caution to the Pilgrim, to keep a tight rein on his eyes, is not only the classic prescription for the control of lust: it also reminds us that the action of this canto, the spirit's obscure preparation for a frightening effort, occurs below either physical or intellectual perception.

In the last quatrain the chief metaphors of the whole canto, and of the preceding terrace of lust—the wound, the burning, and the eating—are combined:

> E questo modo credo che lor basti
>   per tutto il tempo che il foco gli abbrucia:
>   con tal cura convien, con cotai pasti
> che la piaga dassezzo si ricucia.

(And for them, I believe, this mode must do,
  for their whole time in that fire where they burn:
  with such a care as this, and with such food,
in the long run, that wound must be resewn.)

Here too the metaphors (like Virgil's early in the canto) do
not fuse into one sensuous, imaginative whole. I think Dante
did not intend them to ("this mode must do"). As author
he must be content with such inadequate illustrations as he
can find, of an action and passion not to be "expounded in
language." We are coming close to the mystery of purgation,
but the closer we come to it the less adequate our concepts
and metaphors become; and "in the long run" the author
must rely upon the fact itself, and the reader's acquaintance
with it. As the Pilgrim approaches the moment with Beatrice,
where his own human betrayal crashes through the fictive
texture of the poem, revealing author and Pilgrim as one,
the author's make-believe, and his poetic inspiration, grow
thinner. We begin to see through the poem to its historic
meaning for Dante the individual, and to sense in another
way the difference between the shadow and the reality, the
real world and the world of the poem.

ᴣ❧ CHAPTER 18: THE *DOLCE STIL NUOVO*

IT IS IN CANTO XXIV, the second canto devoted to the terrace of the gluttonous, that the Pilgrim meets Bonagiunta da Lucca, and gives him the famous formula for the "sweet new style" of Dante's own poetry. Bonagiunta had belonged to the Sicilian school, and had made fun of Guinicelli, a member of Dante's school, which cultivated the *dolce stil*. Bonagiunta, with the clarity of the afterlife, now hails the Pilgrim for the very poetic mastery he had denied, or failed to see, on earth (line 49):

> "Ma dì s'io veggio qui colui che fuore
>   trasse le nuove rime, cominciando:
>   '*Donne, ch'avete intelletto d'Amore.*' "
> Ed io a lui: "Io mi son un che, quando
>   amor mi spira, noto, ed a quel modo
>   che ditta dentro, vo significando."

> ("But tell me if I see here the maker of
>   those new-found rhymes which with this verse begin:
>   '*Ladies, who have intelligence of love.*' "
> And I said to him: "I am one who, when
>   love breathes in me, take note, and in that mode
>   go signifying, which he dictates within.")

The Pilgrim's words on a topic of burning interest to students of Dante, and no doubt to Dante himself—the nature of his self-conscious, profound, and original poetics—have the laconic under-emphasis, the self-denying lightness, which characterize most of the conversations between poets and sages which we hear during the third Day. Poetry and the Philosophy of Poetry, like the other good things of earthly life, are renounced almost at the moment they are enjoyed. But this renunciation is paradoxical; for just as the ascetic regime of the Golden Age made even acorns "savory with hunger" (Canto XXII, line 149), so the proper valuation of poetry is the source of its true beauty and beautiful truth.

Though Dante describes his poem-making so briefly, the patient reader may learn to see what the formula means by considering its place in the context of the whole journey. The words of the formula for the *dolce stil nuovo* have by this time acquired a wealth of meaning for Pilgrim and reader; and if we are to understand, or "interpret" them adequately, we must consider their place in the developing form of the drama of the Pilgrim's spiritual growth. Of course I am aware that that would be an endless job. But I may illustrate the method with reference to some of the moments of enlightenment in the journey up to this point, which prepare for this description of the author's poem-making.

The immediate context for the formula is the drama of the third Day, in which, as I have tried to show above, the Pilgrim is more or less consciously trying to slake (Canto XXI, line 1)

> La sete natural che mai non sazia,
>   se non con l'acqua onde la femminetta
>   Sammaritana domandò la grazia.

> (The natural thirst which nothing ever sates
>   except that water which the woman of
>   Samaria demanded as a grace.)

The pull of the love of God, half-hidden behind its many signs, is the chief force in this drama. And now the Pilgrim can briefly note that the love which moves him in the journey also moves him to the act of poem-making which is now recording the journey.

Bonagiunta probably does not understand this fully. He had asked about Dante's "style," and the literal effect of the Pilgrim's answer is merely to shift our attention from style in the usual sense of the arts of language, to its source or inspiration, in love. Perhaps, as the editors of the Temple Classics edition suggest, the Pilgrim is reproving Bonagiunta for an idolatrous attachment to the poem as artifact, or for excessive pleasure in the *effects* of poetizing. Almost any conception of love would do, at this point, to make the distinction between superficial versifying and poem-making which is authentic because obedient to the poet's true inspiration, whatever that may be. And Bonagiunta acknowledges (lines 58-60) that his school was, in fact, not obedient to the voice that dictates within.

But the Pilgrim almost knows that by *love* he himself means the love of God. In Canto XXIII both the mysterious trees and the emaciated spirits which appeared to the Pilgrim were half-understood as signs of that same "desire"— the love of God—which led Christ to his sacrifice. The Pilgrim could not have sensed all this until the third Day, because his own spirit was not yet free enough to feel the "thirst" which deeply moved it, and also because God's love did not yet reveal itself in signs, in the actual scene around him. But now he is approaching the living faith which moves Dante the author: that all the loves he has seen and heard, even those of Hell, the creation of *Il Primo Amore*, are analogous because founded in the love of God. So that when he speaks of the dictation of "love" he means the countless analogous voices in which Love has spoken up to this point, and he assumes that, in his further ascent, love will speak in other voices still. We understand "love" as the love of God. But just as the love of God is hidden behind every mode of mortal love, and includes them all, even the Hellish, so Dante's inspiration includes every other authentic source of poetry, and transcends them all. On the way up the Mountain, and in the *Antipurgatorio*, the Pilgrim has felt the force and the truth and beauty of many poetries, ancient and contemporary; but having enjoyed them, has passed on. They were all obedient to love but short of the love of God. And as the Pilgrim enjoys and rejects these forms of poetizing, many classic problems and puzzles of poetic theory are dramatically (if not theoretically) presented—to be resolved, at last, in the notion of divine inspiration which we get so briefly here near the top of the Mountain.

Thus, for instance, when the Pilgrim meets his friend Casella the musician, the two are totally and idolatrously absorbed in the pleasure of Casella's song and Dante's verses (Canto II, line 115):

> Lo mio maestro ed io e quella gente
> ch'eran con lui parevan sì contenti,
> come a nessun toccasse altro la mente.

> (My master then, and I and all the rest
> who were with him, showed forth such happiness
> as though our minds played upon nothing else.)

But moral Cato breaks up their doting session and sends them scudding on their way. It is one of several places where the Pilgrim meets the classic conflict between poetry—however authentic, or true to the particular love that speaks it—and morally responsible action. It is the conflict which made Plato, having honored the poets, send them on their way; the conflict which Tolstoi could not resolve when he discovered, late in life, that art was in itself non-moral. The Pilgrim himself cannot resolve the conflict then; he sees no connection between out-going morally purposed action, and the intense pause of lyric contemplation.

I pointed out in Part One that the Pilgrim's recurrent lyric awareness in the unspeaking, earth-like realm of the *Antipurgatorio* reminds one of a great deal of modern poetry. Part of its beauty is in the feeling it brings that it is deeply significant, but the meaning is only *confuses paroles*: unrelated therefore to any kind of understanding or motivation outside the poetic awareness itself. Professor Maritain has analyzed the practice and theory of modern poets more deeply and clearly than anyone else; and he thinks that the knowledge of poetry in itself which is to be found in their works is unique, an original conquest of the modern spirit. We learn from them that the poet's inspiration is not to be confused with any other mode of the spirit's life, and that his aim, *qua poet*, to make a work of beauty, is also unique. Dante certainly did not explicitly elaborate this doctrine, but in passages like the one with Casella he feels and dramatizes the truth on which it is based. The enchanted enjoyment of Casella's song presents the same mode of the spirit's life— esthetic contemplation—as Shelly's image of the mind as a fading coal, which Stephen Dedalus quotes with admiration: a pause in which one is aware of nothing else.

But the poem in which the poetic focus of the mind is presented does not itself pause: the flight of the friends from Cato's scolding is poetry too. That act of spirit whereby the song was held and enjoyed is accepted as good, but not *the* Good; Cato's scruples, arising from a different orientation of the spirit, are accepted as good, but not as Good itself. The *dolce stil* can flow into each *moto spiritale*, clear and resonant in each successive moment, yet always moving ahead. The contrasting modes of the spirit's life, each with its own poetry, pass before us like colors in a turning spectrum, for the *dolce stil* (as Dante believed) had its source, not in any one of them, but in *their* source: the full white light itself. He thinks of his poetry not as *a* poetry, but *the* poetry: the poetry of poetries, as one might put it.

It was in Canto xviii that Virgil expounded his doctrine of human loves, the motive power of the endlessly-varied forms of life. And at that point I suggested (Chapter 11) that Dante's poetics was akin to Aristotle's. Dante's "love" would correspond to Aristotle's *praxis*, or "action." And the mimetic act of love or sympathy whereby Dante represents the lives of other spirits, would correspond to Aristotle's "imitation of action." The definition of the *dolce stil* emphasizes the poet's *inspiration*, and thus appears to agree with romantic and post-romantic doctrines of poetry as the expression of a feeling. So it does; but because the inspiration comes from outside the poet, there is room for the realism and objectivity of Aristotle's definition also. Dante thought of his poetry as coming from his whole awareness of the whole world: nature, human society, history; and the whole world, in his belief, reflected God. This world had been explored before, and the record of successive explorations was embodied in books of all kinds. That is why he did not fear (as contemporary poets sometimes do) that he would violate his inspiration through study, direct observation, and non-poetic disciplines of the mind and the will. On the contrary, he thought that the world and history, if truly seen, would "dictate" the same thing to him as the inspiration which spoke within. And obedience to Love's voice inside would be the same thing as the mimetic act of love whereby he represented the spirits of those he had known on earth; he mimicked them as they really were, *sub specie aeternitatis.*

Thus I think that Dante's poetics includes something like Aristotle's, but (in his intense faith) goes beyond it. And the new "faith" was necessary; he could not have repeated literally the classic achievement. For on the one hand he lacked the cultural sustenance of Aristotle's Athens or Virgil's Rome, and on the other hand he knew more than they did, he knew the death of their cultures. Only the most general timeless truths of antiquity were available to him, not their actual life. Aristotle's definitions are based on Sophocles' tragedy, which he takes for granted. Virgil, in an analogous way, takes his own refined pagan spirit for granted, and on that basis expounds the timeless principles of the human spirit in *any* body. In the last chapter I mentioned that Statius' account of the soul's life and creative power completes Virgil's: it affirms the God-given power of the individual human spirit; something not to be taken for granted (without reference to the contingencies of history, and as part of nature) but to be explained, by faith, as the special

Grace of God. And Dante had to account for the poetry of
the *Divine Comedy* in a similar way: as due to the love of
God speaking within him, and no one else. Thus his theory
of poetry confirms the classic doctrine of the imitation of
action and the mirror of Nature, but at the same time takes
account of the faith underlying its *re*birth in his own art.

Thus when the Pilgrim tells Bonagiunta that *amor,* speaking within him, is the source of his style, he is thinking of
all the analogous ways in which love may speak to poets.
His first obedient act as poet is to "note" what love says,
receive that love in his own spirit—or, as I think one may put
it, wordlessly *mimic,* in his own love, the love that enters
from without. The second part of the Pilgrim's definition
touches upon the more external (or as Professor Maritain
calls it, *executive* act of the poet), which is more like style
in its usual sense:

> ed a quel modo
> che ditta dentro, vo significando.

He proceeds to signify what he has noted in his own inner
being *in the mode* in which it came to him.

The word "modo" in Dante's usage refers, like "amor,"
to an analogical concept. Sometimes it merely means "way"
or "fashion." Often it means a mode of the spirit's life, a
particular action, as when he speaks of the "modo" of the
lustful repenting in the flame. And in his *Letter to Can
Grande* he mentions ten *modi,* in this case modes or forms
of *discourse,* which are the forms of the poem itself: "The
form or method (*forma sive modus*) of treatment is poetic,
fictive, descriptive, transumptive; and likewise proceeding
by definition, division, proof, refutation, and setting forth
of examples." (Temple Classics edition, par. 9, page 348.)

Professor Curtius has studied the technical meaning of
these ten "modes" in the Logic and Rhetoric of Dante's
time; and he thinks that when Dante offers this list he
does so in full, technical awareness; and, moreover, that he

thereby claims, for *his* poetry at least, a scope which Scholastic theory denied to poetry as such. Dante's list of modes, Professor Curtius points out (page 230) "falls into two groups of five. The first, as we now see, indicates the poetic-rhetorical, the second the philosophic aspect of the work. The phrase *et cum hoc* ['and likewise' in the T. C. translation above] firmly establishes both in a programmatic sense. It means: *my work offers poetry, but at the same time philosophy also.* Thereby Dante claims for his poetry the function as knowledge which the Scholastic theory of poetry had opposed."

This may be another indication that Dante thought his own poetry unique; that it transcended and included, not only various kinds of poetry, but other forms or modes of discourse as well. We have seen that, in fact, the iridescent flow of Dante's style seems to contain all the modes of discourse, from the rational at one end of the spectrum to the most purely metaphorical or poetic at the other—especially when he wishes to show some wide shift in the Pilgrim's inner life, from one stage of awareness to another, as in Canto ix, the beginning of purgation proper.

In terms of the Pilgrim's definition, one would say that love may speak within, sometimes in a rational mode, sometimes in a metaphorical, and sometimes in "examples"—the mode of a particular spirit's being. And the clue to the *dolce stil* is again obedience to that love and its very mode, first as the poet imitates it in his inner being, and then as he imitates it in the poem. Saint Bonaventura traced all the arts and sciences back to theology; Dante traces all the modes of the spirit's life and languages back to the love of God. That is why the poetry of the *Commedia*, however luminous and beautiful in the detail, is never its own end: it always points ahead and beyond its momentary beauty. It has its life between the ever-changing human spirit one way, and the unfathomable mystery of God, the object of faith, the other way. We know that the *Divine Comedy* is not the poem to end all poetries; while there is human life, there is *poetando* of some sort. But the little formula for the *dolce stil nuovo* contains *in nuce* a kind of ideal poetics which, so far as I know, is the most strict, exigent, and all-inclusive theory of the mysterious art of poetry which any-one ever worked out.

Where we read the formula in the poem, its alarming scope is merely implied; and neither the Pilgrim nor Bona-giunta tries to explore such meanings as I have suggested above. Bonagiunta takes it in with becoming awe, and falls silent "as though satisfied" (line 63). As for the Pilgrim, the definition of the poetic mission which awaits him after the journey, is (like everything in this part of the *Purga-torio*) a semi-transparent sign of the Grace of God, now moving him upward faster and faster. Under this pressure he turns away from poetry; and in the next canto (xxv) he is intent upon estimating the power of his own spirit as Statius explains it, and upon the act of faith required.

But in Canto xxvi he meets Guido Guinicelli and Arnaut Daniel, purging their lust in the flame, thinking over their own poetry, and hailing Dante as the master. Dante ac-knowledged both of *them* as masters in the very act of going beyond them, and this is to be understood, I think, in the light of his own transcendent theory of poetry. Guinicelli had written little rhymes of love so sweet that they will last as long as the language; Arnaut is "a better craftsman of the maternal speech." Both of them, like any authentic poets, were obedient to the love that breathed in them, but that love was not Love itself. Guinicelli, perhaps, lent ear to the most Eden-like voice of human love. Arnaut, who wept and sang, and who now sees his inspiration as mad-ness, may have heard that theme of love-as-death which many later poets were to consider the inspiration of all poetry. In their art they attained the utmost refinement; yet now, *sub specie aeternitatis*, when they look at Dante whose poetic inspiration was of a different order altogether, they are like oafish peasants (Canto xxvi, line 67):

> Non altrimenti stupido si turba
> lo montanaro, e rimirando ammuta,
> quando rozzo e salvatico s'inurba.

> (So the dazed mountain-dweller looks around,
> troubled within himself, and so grows mute,
> when, wild and uncouth, he enters town.)

CHAPTER 19. CANTO XXVII:
LOVE'S SACRIFICE

In Canto xxvii Virgil, Statius, and the Pilgrim, leaving the terrace where lust is purged, pass through the wall of flame which guards the approach to Eden. Night overtakes them, and they spend the dark hours among the rocks, like two shepherds with a goat between them. The Pilgrim (the well-guarded goat) dreams of Rachel and Leah, two versions, the Contemplative and Active, of human life in obedience to nature and God. As the light of the final morning dawns, the morning when he will enter Eden itself, he receives Virgil's last commission.

The literal narrative is unusually simple, but (as in Cantos viii and xviii) it contains the main themes of the whole preceding Day's journey, which are now felt as ending and obscurely announcing the morrow. I have suggested that during the whole third Day the Pilgrim, driven by his keen new thirst, was working against time. At this point we begin to see that he has craved to *redeem* time: he is returning, after Hell and the inner divisions of his mind's struggle under Virgil's guidance, to his own earliest time, when through Beatrice he received intimations of immortality in childhood. Parallel to this movement of the Pilgrim's own spirit, are the many signs of the Historic Redemption, under the pagan enlightenment of Rome: the way whereby the race is to return to its lost innocence, Eden or the Golden Age—and so redeem the wicked conflicts and treacheries and delusions of historic time. The Pilgrim tries to proceed with the aid of Virgil's and Statius' philosophy. But what really moves him (and what moved Christ) is not ultimately rationalizable. And now, in Canto xxvii, the Pilgrim himself will have to do something beyond reason; he will have to walk through the fire.

The Pilgrim's immersion in the flame may be regarded

as the sacrifice which the love of Beatrice requires. But Beatrice does not yet appear; Dante's individual ordeal is still to come. In this context "love" is everyman's—it has the vast but inexplicit scope, the tacit analogical references, which the word has in the formula for the *dolce stil nuovo*, discussed in the last chapter. On the one hand, any love, since it is not identical with the moral will which is obedient to reason, requires suffering or sacrifice. The lover's neatly-rationalized ego is split open; he must accept a certain dependence upon an object outside himself and his myth of himself. This we may observe even in the tiniest human loyalties. On the other hand, Love itself was also revealed through a sacrifice, that of Christ on the Cross. In both aspects, the divine and the human, love is impermeable to reason, and throughout the third Day we have noticed that this power, which drives the Pilgrim upward, though it is felt, is hidden. It is not to be understood, though it may be experienced.

You may say that the more the Pilgrim experiences his own movement of love, with the subtle sacrifice which it entails, the more does the sacrifice of Christ vibrate around him. The more sharply the microcosm of his own spirit comes into focus, the more does the macrocosm of human history become significant. And the fainter does the timeless humanism, the reasoned morals and psychology of Virgil and Statius, become.

The opening sequence of the canto establishes the vast scene of the action to follow. Here, high on the purgatorial Mountain, it is near sunset, while noon in India, night in Spain, and morning in Jerusalem (line 2):

> là dove il suo Fattore il sangue sparse

(there where his Creator divulged his blood)

We get an impression of the ceaseless procession of light and darkness over the world; not such light as struck the

Pilgrim in Canto xv, when light touched his mind; nor the unearthly light of the *Paradiso*, but light, alternating with dark, as mortals know it from childhood.

At the same time, behind or beyond the visible cosmos, we are reminded of the shedding of Christ's blood. Perhaps its redness echoes the ruddy flames which we may remember from the last canto, and tacitly confirms the approach of sunset here on the Mountain.

The angel of Chastity (whose appearance marks their leaving the terrace where lust is purged) comes into focus (line 7):

> Fuor della fiamma stava in su la riva,
> e cantava, "*Beati mundo corde*,"
> in voce assai più che la nostra viva.

> (He was standing on the verge of the fires
> and singing, "*Beati mundo corde*,"
> in a voice more vivid far than our choirs'.)

The angel tells them that all who would ascend must cross the flame. And next we see the wincing Pilgrim himself on the very edge of the flame which he must enter (line 14):

> per ch'io divenni tal quando lo intesi,
> quale è colui che nella fossa è messo.
> In su le man commesse mi protesi,
> guardando il foco, e immaginando forte
> umani corpi già veduti accesi.

> (wherefore I became, when I grasped his words,
> like a man who has been laid in the grave.
> Bent over my clasped hands, my gaze I turned
> down to the flame, strongly imagining
> human bodies which I had once seen burned.)

The effect of this swift sequence is to bring the vast suggestions of the cosmic scene suddenly, pathetically (and almost comically) down to the sharpest actuality, as though the camera, starting far away, and with a very wide focus, had been suddenly rushed up to the tiny Pilgrim himself, where he crouches defenseless before his ordeal.

The crossing of the flame which is presented in the next sequence (lines 19-57) was foreshadowed in the perilous passage of Canto xxv, along the edge. Now the very act, which was feared then, is upon us. The Pilgrim has been ascending during the third Day partly by the power of the God-given desire within him, partly by the upward-pointing signs which have surrounded and constrained him: the risen Statius, the mysterious trees, the humane elucidations of his guides. But now he must answer by an act of his own will, not with humane reason but against it, and not with the evidence of his senses but against that also. The question is, what *is* such an action, or *moto spiritale*? In the scene which follows we see it in several analogous forms.

First of 'all Virgil tries to accomplish it (lines 20 ff.). One might have thought that Statius, with his Christian faith, would be called upon in this crisis. But the Pilgrim is shaken to the very foundations of that moral being which Virgil had rescued in the dark wood, and then sustained, nourished, and enlightened; all that has been accomplished on the long road is now at stake. It is both poetically and theoretically right that Virgil, *dolce padre*, should take the lead here again, to offer his aid for the last time.

Virgil is human enough to appeal first to his charge's confidence in him. He reminds him of their ride, on Geryon's back, into the abyss of Hell, when the Pilgrim's faith in him, against all that his senses told him, had not failed. When the Pilgrim makes no move, he tries to appeal to reason, and asks the Pilgrim to prove to himself that the fire will not destroy him, by testing it with a bit of his garment. Finally he invokes that fortitude, cornerstone of the reasoned virtues, which the Pilgrim had once learned from him (line 31):

Pon giù omai, pon giù ogni temenza.

(Now cast aside, now cast aside all fear.)

This plea has its effect, though not the desired effect, upon the Pilgrim. The authority of the moral law of pagan enlightenment (like that of the Mosaic Law of the Old Testament in Saint Paul's interpretation) convicts him before his own conscience (line 33):

Ed io pur fermo e contra a coscienza.

(And I still motionless against my conscience.)

He cannot move ahead, because in this mysterious crisis he is become a child again, and, as so often happens with real children, the mention of virtue merely deepens his stubborn despair.

It is then that Virgil sees how to free the Pilgrim by an act of renunciation of his own. He goes behind his own long role in his charge's progress to the hidden beginning of the whole journey, which is destined to be its end also: the love of Beatrice (line 35):

"Or vedi, figlio,
tra Beatrice e te è questo muro."

("Now see, my son,
between you and Beatrice is this wall.")

The Pilgrim, moving at last, takes the center of the stage (lines 37-42):

Come al nome di Tisbe aperse il ciglio
Piramo in su la morte, e riguardolla,
allor che il gelso diventò vermiglio:
così, la mia durezza fatta solla,
mi volsi al savio duca, udendo il nome
che nella mente sempre mi rampolla.

(As at the name of Thisbe, all but dead,
  to see her Pyramus unclosed his eyes,
  when the fruit of the mulberry grew red:
so then, with all my stubbornness untied,
  I turned to my wise leader, hearing the name
  which always gushes upward in my mind.)

With the moving of the Pilgrim, Virgil is lost to sight. But it is clear that he has made an extra-rational act of loyalty or faith—a sacrifice which his love for his charge demanded—analogous to the Pilgrim's, and more touching and enlightening. He has relinquished his own reasoned principles in favor of a mystery he does not understand. And from one point of view this marks the failure of reason as the ultimate guide to human conduct: we are leaving the gloomy fortitude of *Cato morale* behind us. But from another point of view, Virgil's reason here wins its most impressive triumph: at the height of its achievement it acknowledges its limitations. We are reminded of Virgil's warnings in Canto xviii, when the Pilgrim was too satisfied by his explanation of human loves. And here we see Virgil as Statius saw him: carrying a light which does not benefit him, but will light his followers on beyond him, the image which is the clue to Virgil's role throughout the third Day.

Virgil's sacrifice neither avails him to go ahead, nor destroys his own integrity. When the Pilgrim's paralysis is dissolved by Beatrice's name, he smiles sadly (line 45)

come al fanciul si fa ch'è vinto al pome.

(as one does at a child won by an apple.)

He would have sympathized with the enlightened Greeks mentioned by Saint Paul, for whom the Cross was folly. And his pedagogical method with the Pilgrim—you might call it a trick—is based on the classic rationalist explanation of faith from that day to this: that it is only an illusory substitute for the appetites of the flesh, a disguise of Eros. And certainly his view of the Pilgrim's *moto spiritale* as childish helps us to understand it.

We are to take it that the Pilgrim, faced by such painful mysteries as his own infidelity to Beatrice's love (a sign of human infidelity in general) must in some sense become a child again. But as though to remind us that his obedience is not literally the innocence of childhood but innocence regained, his experience is associated with the ambiguous dying and ambiguous revivification of the mythic Pyramus, as his blood, shed in faithlessness and error, stains the mulberry red. And that blood reminds us, though faintly, of the mystic blood of Christ of line 2. So Dante the author has placed the Pilgrim's *moto spiritale* in the center of the drama, but illuminated it by means of three analogous actions: that of the child bribed by an apple, that of Pyramus finding and losing his mortal human love for Thisbe, and that of Virgil acknowledging the end of his vision like a father who bids his son God's speed. And behind it all is the suggestion of Christ's sacrifice, which will reappear in another way in the pageants and symbolic shows of the *Paradiso Terrestre*, and in still other ways in the *Paradiso*.

But the Pilgrim has yet to meet Beatrice herself; and when he does so, the personal intensity of the sacrifice which her love demands will be such as almost to break the texture of the poem. And the visions of Christ in the *Paradiso* entirely transcend his experience here. The sacrifice of love in this canto does not reach either the divine, or the most intimately individual end of the spectrum. It is the sacrifice which ends the purgatorial journey under Virgil's guidance, revealing its hidden machinery: that subrational or super-rational love-driven dying-to-live, which is both tragic and Christian. It shows this sacrifice in a context which is human (as distinguished from either personal or divine), and human in the widest and richest sense. And it leads to an innocence like that of childhood, like that of Eden, like that of "the first human time," the Golden Age of Virgil's legend.

The travellers' passage through the flame (lines 46-57), with its torture, its music, and Virgil's comforting talk of the beloved woman beyond, is the climax and peripety, the turning point in the *moto spiritale* of the canto as a whole. And the last part of the canto (a prolonged epiphany) shows what moved the travellers through such action and passion: the beauty of earth (which Beatrice the mortal woman epitomizes) reflected in the Pilgrim's cleansed and translucent spirit. We are hardly conscious of leaving the burning, so easily do we become aware of the angel of the stair, and the approach of night (lines 58-63). The last few steps fly past below us, and we come to rest for the dark hours. While night passes over our heads, we pass into dream and out of it without a break, for now the visions which come from the hidden part of the dreamer's psyche, distorted by no inner tensions of his own, agree almost literally with his awakened senses, which take in dawn on the edge of Eden. Virgil's last words, freeing the Pilgrim from the constraints of both ecclesiastical and secular rule, merely describe what he already experiences (lines 127-140).

The last part of the canto has its traditional symbols— Eve's apple, Cytherea, Rachel and Leah in the dream, signs of the contemplative and active life—and they may all be interpreted to show the meaning of the canto in Dante's abstract schemes. And Virgil's final words are full of references to moral and political theory which is built into the whole journey up the Mountain. But the philosophy and the allegory are, as it were, dissolved in the poetry. For Dante wishes to show that innocent love of the transient and eternal beauty of earth which all humans must have, though not at will. And to restore our sense of it he relies upon his lyrical and musical mastery, as he had in the first canto of the *Purgatorio* (line 13):

Dolce color d'oriental zaffiro,
   che s'accoglieva nel sereno aspetto
   dell'aer puro infino al primo giro,
agli occhi miei ricominciò diletto,
   tosto ch'i' uscii fuor dell'aura morta
   che m'avea contristati gli occhi e il petto.

(The tender color of the eastern sapphire
   which was appearing in the tranquil height
   of pure air, as far as to the first gyre,
restored to my eyes once more their delight,
   as soon as I emerged from the dead air
   which had so saddened both my eyes and heart.)

That was early morning on the first Day, and now we are about to leave the beauty of earth altogether. Perhaps for that very reason the return of that feeling is deeper: as memory is better than what we have, and innocence restored is beyond childhood.

The whole end of this canto, echoing the first morning and the first night, suggests the beginning and ending not only of this but of many journeys. It is one of the places where Dante speaks with the most musical directness of *il cammin di nostra vita*, "the journey of our life." We feel it in the coming of night (line 70):

E pria che in tutte le sue parti immense
   fosse orizzonte fatto d'un aspetto,
   e notte avesse tutte sue dispense,

(And before the whole stupendous range
   of the horizon had become one color,
   and night had taken all for her domain,)

We feel it also in the coming of dawn (line 109):

E già, per gli splendori antelucani,
   che tanto ai peregrin surgon più grati
   quanto tornando albergan men lontani

(And in the brightness which precedes the dawn,
   rising more grateful to returning pilgrims
   as their night's lodging is less far from home)

Night and morning, when we are really aware of them, restore our earliest sense of ends which are beginnings and
beginnings which are ends. The night which the Pilgrim
passes like a goat between two shepherds might be the eve
of any initiation, any *rite de passage* between the cradle and
the grave (line 82):

   e quale il mandrian che fuori alberga,
      lungo il peculio suo queto pernotta,
      guardando perchè fiera non lo sperga:

   (and like the shepherd who, outdoors all night,
      spends the dark hours with his flock, on guard
      lest a wild animal put it to flight:)

And in this moment is suggested both the feeling of the
candidate, and that of the guardian, parent, or teacher, who
(as before a commencement or an induction or a first day
at school) knows that he will presently have to say good-
bye. So Virgil does in the new day (line 115):

   "Quel dolce pome, che per tanti rami
      cercando va la cura dei mortali,
      oggi porrà in pace le tue fami."

   ("That sweet apple, which the care of mortals
      goes searching after through so many branches,
      on this day will bring peace to all your hungers.")

We cannot tell whether the apple is Eve's, with its burden
of suffering now to be transcended, or a fruit of the Golden
Age, or even the food of angels. But there is something in
the music of the words themselves which tells us that reach-
ing it will also be a leaving; and we are prepared for Virgil's
almost tacit farewell (line 139):

"Non aspettar mio dir più, nè mio cenno."

("Expect my words no more, nor any sign.")

The narrative of the whole canto, especially after the crossing of the flame, is extremely simple, moving smoothly, almost without breaks: without haste, yet with a kind of hidden excitement like that of speed. This sequence is also song, or lyric, similar in kind to some of the most magical contemporary verse. I am thinking, for instance, of Saint-Jean Perse's *Anabase*, a musical and dreamlike essence of many journeyings. Or of moments in Eliot's *Four Quartets* when the theme, "In my beginning is my end," reaches us most intimately:

> Here, the intersection of the timeless moment
> Is England and nowhere. Never and always.
>   (*Little Gidding*, I.)

By means of such song Dante conveys to us the love that moved the Pilgrim to the sacrifice of the purgatorial journey, not in the light of its final interpretation, but as any mortal, any candidate for the mysterious initiations of growing life, may feel it.

PART FOUR

TIME REDEEMED
(THE MORNING OF THE FOURTH DAY:
CANTOS XVIII-XXXIII)

ᘒᕉ CHAPTER 20. THE DEVELOPED FORM OF THE *PURGATORIO*

THROUGHOUT these studies I have tried to be guided by Dante's words to Can Grande, which I have quoted in several contexts: "The exposition of the letter is nought else than the development of the form." Only by keeping that in mind can one get the life of the poem, which, like other kinds of life, is always moving and changing. And only thereby can one get the meanings the author intended: interpretation is possible only in successive contexts, which define and qualify it; and it is to be reached, therefore, only in successive efforts of understanding.

But now we have come to the *Paradiso Terrestre*, which concludes the whole poem, echoing the *Antipurgatorio* as the epiphany at the end of a Sophoclean tragedy echoes the prologue. In order to get some idea of the *Paradiso Terrestre*, it is necessary to think over the dramatic form of the whole canticle; to consider the parts and their relationships abstractly. For this purpose I have prepared the following diagram (see over) which, I hope, will serve as a convenient summary of the conception of the structure of the *Purgatorio* which I am proposing.

This diagram is divided into four horizontal columns, each devoted to one of the Days of the Journey: the first Day, the *Antipurgatorio*, at the top, and reading downward, the second Day, the third Day, and the fourth morning, in Eden, at the bottom.

The nine vertical columns indicate nine ways of describing the four Days, which are the main parts of the poem. Reading from left to right, the first three vertical columns show the abstract schemes: the division into cantos, the chronology, and the classification of the sins according to Aristotle and Aquinas. The next three columns indicate the changing drama of the Pilgrim's progress, the scenes in

Cantos	Days of the Journey	Classification of Sins	Meaning of Visible Scene for Pilgrim and Reader	Pilgrim's Moto Spirituale	Pilgrim's Guide	Fulfillment of Dante's Own Life	Itinerarium Mentis in Deum	Allegory of Theologians
1-9	First	Saved but unable to begin work of growth	Illegible, like visible world of nature	Lyric aspiration and awareness	Virgil—as omniscient father	Childhood or potentiality of growth	Direction of soul's love is "extra nos"	Toward the Letter (*littera gesta docet*); exploration of scene of earth, short of grace of revelation
	FIRST NIGHT							
9-19	Second	Repenting proud, envious, angry, slothful	The condition of soul under particular sin, i.e., emptiness or darkness	Moral and intellectual effort leading to "Soul's knowledge of itself." Virgil's natural light	Virgil—as coach & then as philosopher & teacher	Growth through abandonment of the *Convivio*	Love's direction "intra nos"	Toward the Trope (*moralia quid agas*); moral content of journey is brought to light
	SECOND NIGHT							
19-27	Third	Repenting avaricious, gluttonous, lustful	Condition of sinful soul & Christ's sacrifice	Effort to transcend mortality or "time," i.e., slake natural thirst which nature alone cannot slake	Virgil—as companion, plus Statius	Age, return to Beatrice from "Lady Philosophy." Pilgrim approaches Author	Love's direction "super nos" via signs of *allegoria*	The allegory (*allegoria quid credas*); we move toward allegory of *Paradiso Terrestre*
	THIRD NIGHT							
27-33	Fourth: dawn to noon	Innocence regained	Human innocence in relation to Fall & Redemption	Immediate obedience to all he perceives	Matelda	Vision of his own and (by analogy) humanity's purgation	"Super nos" but blocked by Letter of Allegory	Letter of Allegory, visible signs of *quid credas*

which he finds himself, the nature and goal of his action, and the nature of the guide who leads him. The last three columns, on the right, indicate three ways of interpreting the meaning: in terms of Dante's (and by analogy every man's) earthly life; in terms of the *itinerarium mentis in Deum* (journey of the soul to God); and lastly, in terms of the medieval fourfold scheme of Scriptural Interpretation.

In these studies I have had very little to say about the first three vertical columns, but a study of the *Purgatorio* which made any pretensions to completeness would have a great deal to say about them. The division into cantos, their division into lines, and their combination into canticles—all of these apparently merely quantitative aspects of the form of the poem—are part of Dante's intricate number symbolism. The time-scheme, the division into Days and Nights, is part of Dante's Christian calendar, and also of his geography, astronomy, and cosmology, all of which are important for the structure of his whole ideal theatre of life beyond the grave. The classification of the sins, of course, involves the traditional philosophy and theology which, in Dante's scheme, is organically connected with the chronology and the number symbolism. The reader who may wish to pursue these matters can find valuable references in any of the standard commentaries.

The next three columns, ways of understanding the drama and poetry of the Pilgrim's spiritual growth, indicate the aspect of the form of the poem with which these studies are chiefly concerned.

The last three vertical columns, on the right, indicate ways of interpreting the poem with reference to actual human life on earth, hence outside the poem. I have mentioned them, from time to time, in the preceding chapters; but now I wish to discuss them a little further. For in the *Paradiso Terrestre*, as the poem ends, its interpretation is provisionally completed also.

One may say (using Professor Auerbach's valuable terms)

that Dante the Pilgrim's journey of purgation is the "fulfillment" or the truth *sub specie aeternitatis* of the earthly life of Dante the author. And this life—both its earthly "figura" and its visionary "fulfillment"—stands by analogy for everyman's. Thus, reading down the seventh column, the Pilgrim's Day in the *Antipurgatorio* "means" childhood, both Dante's and the reader's—literal childhood, or the metaphorical childhood of faith in Saint Paul's words, "I understood as a child." The second Day "means" that period in Dante's adolescence or early manhood when he pursued "my lady philosophy" and experienced the inner divisions of the growing soul, and the paradoxes and evanescent enlightenments of Reason's life and action. This Day also "means" an eternally recurrent phase in everyman's growth. The third Day means Dante's maturity when, with his high pagan culture, he slowly returns to the love of Beatrice which had burst upon him at the beginning of his life, and will now reveal all it meant. What it meant was nothing less than the Christian Creed: it was a God-given sign or figure of the Revelation of Love itself. This Day is also intended to mean a timeless phase of human growth, everyman's, even Virgil's: I shall suggest below that its end, in the *Paradiso Terrestre*, pictures a late "natural sanctity" like that of *Oedipus at Colonus* or *The Tempest*.

The next column indicates the meanings of the successive days in the terms of St. Bonaventura's *Itinerarium mentis in Deum*, "The journey of the soul to God." I owe this reference to Professor Singleton's *An Essay on the Vita Nuova*, where he uses the *Itinerarium* to show what Dante was up to in that very subtle little work. He also elucidates the formula itself: *extra nos, intra nos,* and *super nos* are the successive directions in which the soul's love moves in its search for God. They apply very well to the Pilgrim's *moto spiritale* during the first three Days. Thus in the *Antipurgatorio* he looks naïvely outward (*extra nos*) as a child does, at the delights and perils of the world around him.

During the second Day he looks inward (*intra nos*) endeavoring to understand the sufferings and the true or illusory objects of his own psyche. During the third Day he turns outward again, but all that he sees—the risen Statius, the fragrant trees—are signs and figures pointing upward (*super nos*) to the eternal death and resurrection of Christ. The third Day may thus be regarded as a long turning, or conversion, of the soul, from the inward gaze to the upward gaze, by way of many signs of Christ. And the end of this movement is in the *Paradiso Terrestre*, where the visionary pageant unrolls the historic Christian Creed, man's innocence, fall, and Redemption, pointing by implication upward, to the unimagined beatitude of the *Paradiso*.

The last vertical column on the right indicates an interpretation of the *Purgatorio* according to the medieval method of assigning four meanings to Sacred Scripture, the Literal, the Tropological, the Allegorical, and the Anagogical. Dante briefly defines the Literal and the three "spiritual meanings" in the *Convivio* and again in the *Letter to Can Grande*. The medieval rhyme, often quoted, is convenient:

> Littera gesta docet,
> Quid credas, allegoria,
> Moralia, quid agas,
> Quo tendas, anagogia.

"The Letter teaches us what things were done; the Allegory, what you must believe; what you must do, the moral (or trope); where you should aim, the anagoge." The three spiritual meanings may be thought of as more or less hidden dimensions of actual (literal) human life. The *moralia*, or trope, shows the motive (or action or *moto spiritale*) behind the visible deed. The Allegory shows the relation of this particular deed to History: i.e., its place in the whole ancient social and cultural tradition, which, in the Christian scheme, is intelligible and significant only in relation to the historic event of Revelation. The historic dimension, or the "Allegory," is defined, as *quid credas,* what you must believe; for one's role in history is to be understood only by means of the Creed. The anagoge shows the vertical relation of any and all events to God, the more or less unavowed goal of human life: *quo tendas,* where you should aim.

There is fairly general agreement among students of Dante that the *Divine Comedy* is somehow composed in imitation of Scripture, and with all three spiritual meanings, or dimensions. But there is little agreement about just how this works in detail. And no wonder; for throughout the *Divine Comedy* one may see the movement of understanding moving from the Literal to some aspect of the spiritual meaning, in many figures, both large and small. Thus the *Inferno* as a whole may be regarded as the realm of the Literal, for what the souls do there is all there is, literally, to their separated lives; and because they have lost the good of the intellect, they grasp neither the moral significance, the place in history, nor the relation to God, of what they are doing in the same way forever. Yet the *Inferno* itself has its full meaning, its place in the entire scheme. The *Purgatorio* is apparently devoted to exploring the Trope and the Allegory, and the *Paradiso* to the Anagoge. Yet, on the other hand, the three canticles are not strictly and univocally commensurable; and each has its literal events, its sensuously-present scene, and its more or less hidden significance in the whole design.

When I attempt to apply the scheme of fourfold symbolism to the structure of the *Purgatorio,* therefore, I am not trying to deal with the interpretation of the *Divine Comedy* as a whole. I am considering only this canticle, in its main parts or Days; and only the interpretation which the Pilgrim's spiritual growth unrolls before us. Thus (reading down the last column on the right) he sees in the *Antipurgatorio* a scene like that of earth, as it appears to us in moments of poetic innocence, a scene *literally* clear but of undeclared significance. During the second Day, seeking the clue to human life in the fallible movements of the soul itself, he slowly learns the Trope, or moral meaning of his journey. During the third Day it is gradually borne in upon him that the moral life itself can only be realized in a historic context. He feels the ghostliness, for him, of Virgil's and Statius' Rome, whose light had led him; and at the same time the pull of the Creed which can interpret these historic distances, and thereby vivify the present. The end of this sequence, the dawn of the allegorical meaning, is not in the third Day, but in the final morning in Eden. There the terrible and marvellous meaning of his own life in his own Italy strikes him with full force; and there the meaning of History is visible in the Divine Pageant. And both visions (or both complementary aspects of the one allegorical meaning) are due to Beatrice, at once type or *figura* of Christ, and the woman whose love convicted and saved Dante himself.

It will be noticed that each successive level of interpretation in Dante's developing form, assumes and includes the one below. When the Pilgrim learns during the second Day to understand the movements of his aspiring love, he can assign some meaning to the literal earthly scene. When during the third Day he learns the sacrifice of faith, he has (in his being, if not in his mind) the clue to his moral growth now largely behind him. That is why the *Paradiso Terrestre* corresponds to the *Antipurgatorio* as the epiphany ending a tragic action corresponds to its prologue, and why the approach to Eden recalls the beginning of the journey, mingling homecoming with leave-taking. The journey may be understood as a series of revisions, each wider than the one before, of the one underlying action, "to course over better waters," as the first words of the canticle describe it.

The comparison between the *Antipurgatorio* and the *Paradiso Terrestre* throws some light on both. The Pilgrim grasps the earthly scene at the beginning of the journey with poetic innocence, and the visions of Eden and Redemption with the naïveté of faith. Both the earthly scene and the scene of Eden contain meanings which the mind does not grasp, and in this respect both contrast with the second and third Days, when intellectual insight grows and then fades out, giving place to the act of faith. In the *Antipurgatorio* Dante the author is farthest from the Pilgrim, who is just beginning to explore what the author has been through. Yet the author, as he writes, is on our earth like any other man, and in this respect he is close to the earthlike experience of the Pilgrim. In the *Paradiso Terrestre* the author knows that he is completing only one canticle; the *Paradiso* is to follow; and so the distance between him and the Pilgrim may be felt again, and vaster than ever. But the author, like the Pilgrim, can see no more on the basis of the journey which *this* poem records. He too is paralyzed by the hard Letter of the Creed, and in this respect he is identical with the Pilgrim, he can understand no more.

Thus the *Paradiso Terrestre* ends the *Purgatorio*, tying-off its countless interwoven themes, and bringing its *moto spiritale* to a halt. But the journey has brought us only to the third level in Dante's fourfold scheme of symbolism: the Allegory, *quid credas*. And *its* meaning, the Anagoge, is unimaginable here. That will be the theme of the *Paradiso* for which Dante the author will prepare a new basis entirely. In a study of the whole *Divine Comedy*, the *Paradiso Terrestre* might be regarded as the prologue to the *Paradiso*. But such a conception would have to be surrounded with many qualifications, just because of the fundamental mutation, the inexplicable change of life, which Dante indicates between the two canticles. In the three chapters which follow, I make no attempt to study the ultimate meanings which Dante may have hidden in the vision of Eden. I wish only to suggest a reading of that vision as the end of the purgatorial journey, and of the poem which records it.

WE LEARN in the beginning of the *Inferno*, in Canto I by
covert reference, in Canto II very explicitly, that Beatrice is
the efficient cause of Dante's whole journey back to God.
This applies both to the author's life, and to the vision which
the poem records; for Beatrice, like Dante himself, is both
inside the poem and outside it: both the Florentine girl who
died (a *figura*) and the fulfillment of that earthly life which
we see at the end of the *Purgatorio*, and, in other ways in
the *Paradiso*. Her appearance, therefore, in Canto XXX, in
the center of the *Paradiso Terrestre*, is the answer to a long
expectation which the plot of the *Commedia* has aroused in
the reader. The arc of suspense, as one might put it, stretches
from the very beginning in the Dark Wood to its anchor in
the vision of Eden.

Her appearance in Canto XXX is also the end of a smaller
arc, stretching from Canto XVIII (when Virgil ended his account of the soul's life in the light of reason with a reference
to Beatrice's higher wisdom) through the whole third Day,
to earthly felicity itself. Virgil revealed the Trope, the moral
meaning of spiritual growth; Beatrice's appearance will show
its basis in love and faith, *quid credas*, the allegorical meaning of all that the Pilgrim has done and suffered and seen.

We are reminded of her briefly in Virgil's last words on
the threshold of Eden (Canto XXVII, line 136):

> "Mentre che vegnan lieti gli occhi belli,
>   che lagrimando a te venir mi fenno,"

> ("While the fair eyes in joyfulness are coming,
>   which in their weeping made me come to you,")

and so the opening cantos of the *Paradiso Terrestre*, XXVIII
and XXIX, make a shorter and more intense arc ending in her

actual appearance. This places the Pilgrim's marvellous and terrible meeting with her, Cantos xxx and xxxi, in the middle of Eden; and after that the vision is broken, and all movement gradually comes to a stop.

I have remarked that the *Paradiso Terrestre* as a whole may be regarded as a set-piece ending the purgatorial drama: the Creed (or *Symbole*, as it is called in French) made visible. This mysterious phenomenon *is* innocence. But it is innocence regained, and therefore the Fall, the Redemption, and the historic vicissitudes of Revelation on earth, must somehow be contained in the rainbow pageantry of peace-on-earth. To pack all this into a few cantos, unrolling it all with the smoothness of the vividest dream, is an extraordinary feat of poem-making, even for Dante's genius, and even with all the resources of figural and symbolic shorthand which he possessed. The erudite are still exploring the theology, the scriptural interpretation, and the myths and rites of various peoples which went into his visions of Eden. I do not attempt to deal with these allusions, and for that reason I do not offer analyses of particular cantos or passages. I wish to consider the main parts of the morning in Eden, the succession of visions of which Beatrice is the center.

Coming a little closer to the poem, one sees that it is not so much one vision of earthly felicity as a series of visions whose inner coherence we do not grasp. Taken together, they present an experience which is in essence paradoxical.

In Canto xxviii, when the Pilgrim enters Eden with the rising sun, and sees Matelda across the clear stream of Lethe, we feel, as yet, no contradictions. This canto all moves within the high humane awareness of the end of the third Day, Virgil's and Statius', and it shows us Eden as a timeless pole of human experience, an intuition found in the legends of many peoples. Virgil knew it as the *primo tempo umano*, the first human time, the Golden Age. The canto ends with a reference to this classical legend; and Virgil's answering smile (line 146) is almost the last we see of him.

But in Canto xxix we see the beautiful woods lit up as though by lightning, and in this light, which anomalously stays and grows, the majestic procession of Revelation's historic unfolding, from the prophets of the Old Testament to the triumphal car of Christ, stretches along the stream before us and comes to a halt. The light effects alone, in which the natural beauty of Eden as we first saw it fades, make a sharp break between one vision and the other. The shift is, no doubt, from the Trope to the Allegory; from Eden as the timeless goal of all human moral effort, to Eden as historically reconstituted by Redemption: *quid credas.* We have seen this movement from Trope to Allegory in many small figures throughout the third Day, as I explained when discussing the risen Statius and the fragrant trees. But there every effort was made to smooth the shift, to get as much of it as possible into Virgil's and Statius' philosophy; while here the startling arbitrariness of the vision is sharply stressed; the break between reason and faith, nature and the supernatural, comes with the flash of light.

When the pageant has halted across the stream, with the car drawn by Christ the griffon directly opposite the Pilgrim, Beatrice appears in the car (Canto xxx, line 22 ff.). Professor Singleton has explained the dramatic form of this sequence, and the intricate meaning which it reveals, with great elegance and clarity. The reader who wishes to understand this crucial part of the *Commedia*—a beautiful instance of Dante's visionary, symbolic, and dramatic style—should consult Professor Singleton's essay. In the meantime I offer some general observations based on his analysis.

The pageant, as it gradually unrolled its length before the Pilgrim, has presented the coming of Revelation *in history*: the "progressive Revelation of God," as some modern theologians put it. We have seen that this was foreshadowed during the third Day, especially in the development of the symbols of the fragrant trees, which were understood first as nature, and then as signs of Christ. Now we see the historic sequence in visible figures, literally clear to the eye in the pure colors of the spectrum; and it halts with the Griffon and his car before us. The movement of the procession gave us time in its passage: now, in the Griffon, we get its end and transcendence. For the Incarnation is both the "point of intersection of time and eternity" and the end of time in another sense, the figure of the Second Coming and Last Judgment. And it is in this appalling context that Beatrice appears, brought to the Pilgrim by the mysterious Beast of two natures who draws the car. What, then, does Beatrice mean?

Professor Singleton is certainly right, I think, in saying that Beatrice means Christ. She is a type, or figure of Christ, a sign pointing to Him as the Prophets of the Old Testament did; as we have seen that even Virgil and Statius did during the third Day. The other meanings which have been found in her—Love, Divine Wisdom, the Way to God, even the ideal notion of a Visible Church—are all more or less rationalized aspects of that meaning, or, more accurately, that analogical reference. The person, Beatrice, made possible (or, as we saw, *brought*) by Christ, refers to that person as to her ultimate meaning, as the risen Statius did in a more pale and ghostly way. She thus ends the quest of the third Day, a movement of spirit within and against the temporal. She ends also the larger journeys of Dante the man and of Dante the Pilgrim; for she played a role in Dante's individual history analogous to that played by Christ in the history of the human race; and for that reason she can reveal Christ's meaning as it were to Dante's *life* itself. No wonder everything stops for the timeless "moment" which follows. The Pilgrim is to face the beginning and the end of his spirit's life; he is to be both judged and redeemed: in his own being a tiny but burning focus of human destiny.

What he feels is the unintelligible, wounding force of love (Canto xxx, line 43):

volsimi alla sinistra col rispitto
  col quale il fantolin corre alla mamma,
  quando ha paura o quando egli è afflitto,
per dicere a Virgilio: "Men che dramma
  di sangue m'è rimaso, che non tremi;
  conosco i segni dell'antica fiamma."

(I turned me toward the left, with trust as clear
  as the child's who to his mother runs in haste
  when he is hurt, or when he has some fear,
to say to Virgil: "Less than a single grain
  of blood is left in me which does not tremble:
  I know the tokens of the ancient flame.")

But Virgil is gone for good. The wound is too deep for
Virgil's or anyone's philosophy; it reduces Dante to the immediate truth of his own being. And now, for the first and
only time, Beatrice calls him by name, "Dante" (line 55), as
though to wake him and us from the dream of the vision and
the poem. Dante the Pilgrim and Dante the mortal man are
one; Beatrice the woman and Beatrice the sign of Christ
are one; and the love which shakes Dante's humanity is one
with the *Primo Amore* which creates Hell.

This moment (that of the greatest personal intensity in
the whole *Commedia*, as Mr. Eliot points out) is held, while
the procession of time and the forward movement of the
poem are paralyzed, until Dante faints (Canto xxxi, line 88).
In this aspect of eternity Beatrice recalls Dante's promise,
recorded in the *Vita Nuova*, and his faithlessness, of which
the *Odes* and the *Convivio* are the remaining signs. She
does so with the most painful and literal simplicity, sparing
Dante no humiliation, and using all the "venom" (Canto
xxi, line 75) of a full earthly woman who has been betrayed.
The beautiful scene around them and the angelic presences
who "have their vigils in eternal day" and do not know the
cruelty of Love in the human flesh, sharpen the savagery of
the scene. It has some of the quality of modern fiction when

it endeavors to present some painful moment of human experience without understanding or perspective. And, in fact, that is what Dante intends: he wants to give the Letter of his betrayal in sharpest conjunction with what was betrayed.

Though this marks the most burning point of Dante's personal experience, it corresponds to other climaxes in the upward struggle which led to it. It was, for example, foreshadowed in the Pilgrim's paralysis on the edge of the flame (Canto XXVII) when, against his conscience, he could not make the sacrifice which everyman's love or loyalty requires. And the scene as a whole, the end of the purgatorial journey, corresponds to Cocytus, the bottom of Hell, where love is paralyzed in the ice of treachery for good. This correspondence may be traced in various ways in the structure of the three canticles. It may also be felt more directly in some of the sensuous metaphors. In *Inferno* XXXII, line 46, we read,

> gli occhi lor, ch'eran pria pur dentro molli,
> gocciar su per le labbra, e il gelo strinse
> le lagrime tra essi, e riserolli.

> (their eyes, which before were only moist within,
> welled up at the lids, and the cold constrained
> the tears between them, and closed them up again.)

This image prepares the terrible narrative of Ugolino in the next canto, in which our pity, which might bring relief, is frozen by terror. When Dante is paralyzed by Beatrice's truth-of-love, we read (Canto XXX, line 85):

> Sì come neve tra le vive travi
> per lo dosso d'Italia si congela,
> soffiata e stretta dagli venti schiavi,
> poi liquefatta in sè stessa trapela,
> pur che la terra, che perde ombra, spiri,
> sì che par foco fonder la candela:

così fui senza lagrime e sospiri
    anzi il cantar di quei che notan sempre
    retro alle note degli eterni giri.

(As the snow among the living rafters
    along the back of Italy congeals,
    squeezed by the Slavonian winds and blasted,
then in itself all melted downward seeps,
    when the earth, its shadow lost, respires,
    so that it seems a candle melting in heat:
so without tears was I and without sighs
    before the song of those whose notes are tuned
    after the notes of the eternal gyres.)

And the thawing of the heart which will soon end the
scene is given in related imagery (Canto XXXI, line 13):

Confusione e paura insieme miste
    mi pinsero un tal "sì" fuor della bocca,
    al quale intender fur mestier le viste.
Come balestro frange, quando scocca
    da troppa tesa, la sua corde e l'arco,
    e con men foga l'asta il segno tocca:
sì scoppia'io sott'esso grave carco,
    fuori sgorgando lagrime e sospiri,
    e la voce allentò per lo suo varco.

(Confusion and terror mingled together
    forced a "yes" forth from my opened jaws,
    whose meaning only the sight could render.
As a cross-bow will break, when it is launched
    under too great a strain, both string and bow,
    and the arrow touch its mark with less force:
so I burst open under that heavy load,
    disgorging a rush of sighs and of tears,
    and my voice in its outward passage broke.)

When Dante comes to himself after the swoon which ends
the scene with Beatrice, he finds that Matelda has plunged
him into Lethe, the stream which washes away all painful
memories. During the rest of the morning in Eden, as he
slowly accompanies Beatrice, he has four visions separated
by breaks or shifts of awareness, four complementary aspects of earthly felicity.

The first of these is of Beatrice herself, now no longer
obscured by his terrible self-awareness, for Lethe has re-
moved it. He gazes in Beatrice's eyes, and there he sees
Christ the griffon reflected (Canto xxxi, line 121):

> Come in lo specchio il sol, non altrimenti
>   la doppia fiera dentro vi raggiava,
>   or con uni, or con altri reggimenti.
> Pensa, lettor, s'io mi maravigliava
>   quando vedea la cosa in sè star queta,
>   e nell'idolo suo si trasmutava.

> (Exactly as the sun shines in a mirror
>   the double beast within gave forth its rays,
>   now in the one, now in the other nature.
> Consider, reader, if I was amazed
>   when I saw the thing in itself stay quiet,
>   and in the image of itself it changed.)

As Beatrice in the poem is the fulfillment of Beatrice the
woman of Florence, so Christ the griffon is here the fulfillment of this risen Beatrice. But the human mind cannot
take in the divinity and humanity of Christ simultaneously
—nor the mixture of human and divine in Beatrice, or in
any or every man. That is why the successive visions of
Eden, man reconciled to God, are of such immediate brilliance but unfathomable coherence.

The second vision begins in Canto xxxii, when Dante
turns from Beatrice's eyes to the divine procession, which is

now moving again. The paradoxical change of focus is marked in line 13:

> ma poi che al poco il viso riformossi
> (io dico al poco, per rispetto al molto
> sensibile, onde a forza mi rimossi)

> (But when upon the small my sight reformed
> (small, I mean, with respect to the great object
> of perception, from which by force I turned))

The change is from the greater vision of Christ in Beatrice's eyes, to the lesser vision of Christ in human history; but we are to reflect, I think, that in ways beyond our grasp the two are the same. The first slow appearance of the procession, bringing Beatrice, had stopped with Christ's coming; now it approaches the tree in the midst of Eden, which is dry and withered. This tree was announced by the trees in the terrace of gluttony. Here it may be the Tree of the Knowledge of Good and Evil, perhaps also the Tree of Life; almost certainly a symbol of obedience, and hence of Empire, the order of human society. Christ the griffon attaches his car to the "widowed bough" (Canto xxxii, line 50) and at once the whole tree puts forth springlike foliage and flowers. The moment corresponds to those moments in the preceding vision when Dante, forgetting his own faithlessness, was able to see Beatrice in her beauty. What he sees here is apparently a vision of the relations of Church and State, not as they are, but as they ought to be, in the time which follows Christ's coming. They are no more actual, on earth, than the beauty of Beatrice; but Dante has made both visions "real" in the music and imagery of his verse.

This vision ends (Canto xxxii, line 67) as Dante's strength fails again, and he sinks into a mysterious sleep. He wakes to the third vision, which apparently presents, not the ideal but the actual destiny of Christ's Revelation in human history since His coming. The commentators have expounded the theory of history which is figured in this scene: Dante's understanding of the relations between the Church and the secular powers down to his own day. Eden is empty, except for Beatrice, sitting disconsolately under the tree. The Griffon is gone, and now the car is violated by an Eagle, a Fox, and a Dragon; and then by a Harlot and a Giant, who kisses the Harlot and beats her. It is a vision of desolation, treachery, lust, violence, and stupidity; and it ends as the nightmare figures disappear in the woods, leaving them empty again.

The fourth and final vision is presented in Canto xxxiii, the last canto of this canticle. We return to Dante, now Pilgrim and author in one, surrounded by the incomprehensible signs of earthly felicity, and weighed down by the responsibility which his destiny and his vision have imposed. I shall return to Canto xxxiii in the last chapter, for it contains many indications of the style and the interpretation of the whole end of the *Purgatorio*.

The purpose of this very general survey of the chief parts of the morning in Eden is to show that the vision of Beatrice is the center of all its complementary appearances. This vision is implied in the timeless scene of the Golden Age with which the experience of Eden begins, and then made actual by means of the gradual coming, in human history, of Christ's Revelation. She is the betrayed way to God in Dante's own life; and then, after the personal Hell which her appearance brings him (echoing the Infernal vision of Cocytus), she reveals her beauty as Dante's way once more, and, thereby, the paradoxical Way Itself: Christ as both God and Man. She is thus the clue to the interpretation of man's tragic history from the coming of Christ to the present, in Dante's own Europe; and finally she gives Dante his hard instructions, both as man and as the poet of the poem we are reading.

It has been pointed out (notably by Professor Singleton)

that the role which Dante assigns to Beatrice may be considered blasphemous, unless one pays close attention to the *way* in which she is presented. The *vision* of Beatrice is the center of the *Paradiso Terrestre*, which itself presents the allegorical meaning of the whole journey of this life, *quid credas*, what one must believe, or have faith in. As a real woman who lived and died, she can "mean" that to Dante, a real man who lived and would die. But here in Eden, the meaning which she brings is inexplicit: it is packed into the separate and even contrasting visions which surround her, as well as into her mysterious appearance itself. The vision of Beatrice, given in several different aspects, is only the center of the shifting visions of earthly felicity, as perpetually lost and found again, whose ultimate coherence is beyond us. Dante is showing *quid credas*, and, with his incomparable candor and exactitude, he carefully distinguishes belief in its painful and joyful innocence from understanding. He presents the Letter of Beatrice as the center, for him, of the Letter of the Allegory. The interpretation of this literal allegory is in the *Paradiso*; and just as it took the whole journey from the Dark Wood, where Virgil first literally appeared to the Pilgrim, to the end of the second Day of the *Purgatorio* to interpret his meaning, so it will take most of the *Paradiso* to interpret the Beatrice who here literally appears. Toward the end of that entirely different journey the distinction between the faith which availed Dante, and the faith which it led to, will be presented in many ways. Fortunately these matters are beyond the scope of this study.

Meanwhile the *Paradiso Terrestre* has a great deal to offer the contemporary reader besides its allegory. It presents in the images and music of its beautiful verse a mode of human life which other poets have seen in their ways. And in the strange figure of Matelda, Dante's guide in Eden, it offers a dramatic means of understanding this mode of life, and also the literal and visionary style which presents it.

ঌ CHAPTER 22. THE POETRY OF THE END OF THE EARTHLY JOURNEY

THE ART of the *Paradiso Terrestre* is extraordinarily intricate and conscious. But it would be a mistake to conclude therefore that one can in no sense enjoy or understand it before one has figured out the philosophy packed into its elaborate symbolism. One may also listen to its poetry, and so learn to hear more directly (though with the uncertainties of one's own inner ear) what Dante is saying. He is always saying something about a human experience, a mode of life, which he has known. And he always wants the reader to recognize that first, and only then proceed to the interpretation of the symbols, the meaning which his philosophy and his creed assign to that experience.

That is the principle I have tried to use in all these readings. But the *Paradiso Terrestre*, I think, offers special difficulties to us, and not only because it presents the unfamiliar Letter of the unfamiliar allegorical meaning of the whole *Commedia*. Few of us have, or can recognize, the experience which informs this poetry: we have not heard what "love, within, dictates in that mode." And so the *poetry* may be hard for us in our time; for what Dante says in the *Paradiso* (Canto I, line 71):

l'esemplo basti
a cui esperienza grazia serba.

(let the example suffice him
to whom grace vouchsafes the experience)

applies to all poetry, and the more strongly the more rare the experience is. But Dante also knew (none better) that though grace alone can give the experience, poetry may closely echo it, and so lead the reader, by a sympathetic movement-of-spirit like that of deep make-believe, to become aware of analogies, however faint, in what he himself has experienced. And some of these experiences of the reader's have been revealed to him by other poetry he has read. Hence Dante's allusive methods, and hence, when we try to talk about poetry itself—the living work in its direct impact—we inevitably resort to comparisons.

Thus it may help to reflect that the *Paradiso Terrestre* resumes, though in a new way, the inspiration of Dante's earliest verses, which themselves were of the Tuscan school of the *dolce stil*. It may help, that is, if one can get a smell of the fragrance of the *Vita Nuova*, and of the songs of the friends of Dante's youth. I suppose that Mr. Ezra Pound, in *The Spirit of Romance, An Attempt to Define Somewhat the Charm of the Pre-Renaissance Literature of Latin Europe*, has done more than anyone else to make this poetry accessible to us. There are other studies which are much firmer and clearer intellectually than Pound's. But none that I know is so directly concerned with explaining the poetry itself to a reader of English; and there is no point in trying to make a substitute for Pound's beautiful and technically knowing attempt to "define a charm." Suffice it to say that in the Italian poetry of Dante's school, "a cult of the harmonies of the mind," as Pound puts it, there was an *Édénique* inspiration, manifested in many forms. When, for example, Guido Cavalcanti writes, in his seventh sonnet, the line so much admired by Pound:

Che fa di clarità l'aer tremare,

And making the air to tremble with a bright clearnesse,

(Pound's translation), he was reflecting an experience which, in its immediacy, was like Dante's, though Guido was to interpret it quite differently, and never explore its implications so deeply. Such clarity—a harmony of the mind and of the senses, or rather of the mind *in* the senses, is in our first impressions of the *Paradiso Terrestre* (Canto XXVIII, line 7):

Un'aura dolce, senza mutamento
   avere in sè, mi ferìa per la fronte
   non di più colpo che soave vento,
per cui le fronde, tremolando pronte,
   tutte e quante piegavano alla parte
   u' la prim' ombra gitta il santo monte;

(A sweet breeze with no changefulness within
   itself, upon my brow was touching me
   with strength no greater than a gentle wind,
in which the leaves, a-tremble eagerly,
   were turning each and every one toward where
   the holy mountain shadows earliest.)

Of course Dante's own voice, not identical with anyone
else's, may be heard in his poetry from first to last. But by
the time of the *Commedia* it had acquired new tones, new
resources which further distinguish it from the other voices
in his school. For one thing, Dante's inner power had been
clarified and expanded by what he got from his great love
and long study of Virgil and all that Virgil meant. He was
well aware that this distinguished him from the other *stil
novisti*. When the Pilgrim, rehearsing the author's earthly
life in vision, meets Guido Cavalcanti's father in Hell, and
the old man, in deepest grief, asks why his son is not here
too on the journey of genius, the Pilgrim replies (*Inferno*,
Canto x, line 61):

Ed io a lui: "Da me stesso non vegno:
   colui, che attende là, per qui mi mena,
   forse cui Guido vostro ebbe a disdegno."

(And I to him: "Not of myself I came:
   he who awaits me there is leading me;
   perhaps your Guido held him in disdain.")

When the author of the *Commedia* wrote those lines, he
knew that his early inspiration, now returning under the

guidance of Virgil's spirit, had been transformed. He felt already that epic serenity and amplitude, at once impersonal and humane, which one may hear most clearly during the third Day high on the Mountain, and in the first canto (xxviii) of the *Paradiso Terrestre*. And that "classical" aspect of his mature style is more akin to the spirit of St. Thomas Aquinas and to the spirit of Giotto than to the lyric poets of his time.

A great deal of what Mr. André Malraux has to say about Giotto's art applies by close analogy to the poetry of the high Mountain and the threshold of Eden. He writes: "Medieval art had been the first great individualistic art; Giotto's types ceased to have anything individual. The divine seal which Gothic stamped on every face was now being replaced by idealization, by grace of which every face tends to the divine. Idealization reappears whenever man has come to terms with destiny; at Olympia as at Rheims, at Rheims as at Padua, at Padua as in China during the T'ang period. . . . This [the unindividualized idealization] explains why we hear so much about 'Antiquity' in appraisals of Giotto. But what Antiquity is meant? Such Roman remains as he knew bespoke an art opposed to his. . . . No, the only antique art he recalls is that of Olympia and Delphi, with which he joined hands without ever having set eyes on it." Dante did have Virgil, and other ancient texts, and to them, as we saw, he gave full credit. Yet the classical aspects of Dante's style are of course not literally Virgilian; and the general principle that Mr. Malraux uses in explaining Giotto—that his classicism was a matter of a new, analogous attainment and not of copying—applies also to Dante. "So long as the great movement reconciling man with God—and both of them with the world—had not taken place, none of the Rheims discoveries was possible; man did not need anatomy, but theology," Mr. Malraux writes, "to restore to life that slumbering population of ancient statues, all that was required was the dawn of the first smile upon the first medieval figure."

If Dante can see Matelda across the stream of Lethe, it is because he has returned to a moment of human experience which Virgil knew. If Virgil can see her, it is because he had seen what reappears now, after so many centuries of inhumanity (Canto xxviii, line 40):

> una donna soletta, che si gia
>   cantando ed iscegliendo fior da fiore,
>   ond'era pinta tutta la sua via.

> (A solitary lady, who went along
>   singing and selecting flowers from those flowers
>   wherewith her pathway there was all adorned.)

Matelda is an "idealized" figure in Mr. Malraux's sense: she is free of all individual anguish, yet delicately human, a spirit and an image of reconciliation so simple as to be beyond obedience. She has the charm—call it fragrance, or music—of Dante's New Life, but also of Virgil's *primo tempo umano*. She is like one of Giotto's humane angel-figures, both classical and Christian. Virgil gives her that smile of recognition which Mr. Malraux mentions, a smile which he sees echoed in arts from times and places which Dante never dreamed of, the smile which expresses the rare feeling of peace on earth.

But Virgil's smile is the last we see of him (except his bewilderment at Revelation); and for the poetry which gives us the later aspects of the *Paradiso Terrestre*, a music new even for Dante, it is hard to find close parallels. Mr. Malraux points out that Giotto's idealized but humanly-living art emerged from the first *individualized* art. So does the *Paradiso Terrestre* arise out of the chiaroscuro of the soul divided against itself, which we saw in the central cantos of the *Purgatorio,* and below that, out of the agonized individuality of the lost and separated souls in Hell. That is why the comparison with Giotto is appropriate chiefly for the poetry of Eden's threshold. But in the center of Eden itself we are made to remember all that went before, as though to make its beauty more piercing by contrast, or to take up the early discords again, even in the concluding harmonies. I do not know that there is any way actually to understand such effects as these. In their controlled energy (controlling violent contrast) they are full of the unique or Dantesque sense of a mystery at once ineffable and sharply present. (Canto xxxii, line 61):

> Io non lo intesi, e qui non si canta
> l'inno che quella gente allor cantaro,
> nè la nota soffersi tutta quanta.

> (Here is not sung, I did not understand
> the canticle which then that people hymned,
> nor its full melody did I withstand.)

So Dante writes of the unheard music which accompanies the springlike flowering of the withered tree in the midst of Eden, when the Griffon's car is attached to it.

If one takes the hint from Dante himself, abandoning both the music of the verse and the allegorical meaning carried by the symbols, we still have the scene and the dramatic themes of his Eden, and they also point to what he found at the end of the earthly journey. The scene is, if not earth, the beauty of earth. The Pilgrim returns to it, to be reconciled, after the struggles and passions of life. There he meets a childlike figure, a girl, Matelda, who reminds him of his childhood and the childhood of the race. He also meets another female figure whom he has betrayed, but who now forgives him: Beatrice. And in most piercing contrast to the innocence of the scene are nightmare figures of treachery, violence, and lust, which touch his unhealed wounds, and reawaken his own fear and savagery. If one thinks over these elements thus, in general terms, one can see that Sophocles and Shakespeare saw them too, in their different ways, at the ends of their earthly journeys.

We see the old Oedipus, at Colonus, in a sacred grove. The gentle girl, Antigone, his daughter and sister, is his guide; and here he must face, for the final reckoning, the Eumenides, female spirits of fertility and peace, whom his whole being has offended, but who now forgive him. Envoys from Thebes recall the old man's most painful struggles, and the unforgivable treacheries he has suffered. For his mysterious going-off there is music and thunder suggesting Divinity behind nature: present, though unseen.

Both Dante the Pilgrim and the old Oedipus revisit their innocence with all their human savagery, their capacity for hatred, lust, and violence, intact. It is important, I think, not to lose this element in the poetic conception of the *Paradiso Terrestre*—the more so since the familiar pre-Raphaelite reflections of it are so unrelievedly sweet: at best decorative, at worst vapid. Even Charles Williams in his *Figure of Beatrice* (where he attempts to assimilate Dante to Wordsworth) tends to lose the terror which is the wonderful distinction of Dante's beauty, and he leaves us with something too much like the Victorian Ideal of Female Purity.

In Shakespeare's late plays these scenes and these themes recur, and with a frightening mysteriousness comparable to Dante's. They are first clearly heard, perhaps, at the end of *King Lear*, in the juxtaposition of the wheel of fire with Cordelia's innocence. I am thinking also of the Edenlike scenes of earth (very inadequately described as "pastoral") in *Cymbeline* and *The Winter's Tale*—scenes which owe so much of their poetry to the scenes of treachery, jealousy, and hatred which they follow. I am thinking of Marina, Perdita, Imogen, Miranda, and Cordelia, whose roles are parallel to those of Antigone and Matelda. I am thinking, of course, especially of *The Tempest*, for both its themes and its style are oddly but unmistakably akin to the narrative and the drama of the *Paradiso Terrestre*. The masquelike style of *The Tempest*, clear to the eye, the ear, and the feelings, but not to the mind; the classic idealization of some of the figures, especially Ferdinand and Miranda; the evil (treachery) which breaks the pageant, filling Prospero with pain and anger; the scene of earth's beauty, visible to the Utopian Gonzalo, but turning dry and brown when Alonso's courtiers disdainfully eye it—these and many other elements tell us that, in *The Tempest*, Shakespeare is signifying a mode of love's dictation analogous to that which Dante heard at the summit of the stairway.

It may be (as Colin Still suggests in *The Timeless Theme*) that Sophocles, Dante, and Shakespeare were all obscurely aware of very ancient ritual and mythic representations of the journey of earthly life, and of the natural sanctity which those enjoy who survive to the end. Possible common sources may be traced in the literary and even ritual traditions which rather flimsily link the Renaissance, the Middle Ages, and Classical Antiquity. Such studies might provide a kind of collateral evidence in support of the parallels I am suggesting —or they might not. But what we are trying to understand is the poem itself, for there are many who read about the old rites and myths but few who know their meaning in their own experience.

It appears that since *Ash Wednesday* Mr. T. S. Eliot has been seeking to locate this mode of being and awareness in *his* experience, for his poetry since then has contained many themes and images derived both from late Shakespeare and from Dante. One of the clearest of such poems (and to my ear, one of the most beautiful) is *Marina*, the title being the name of that daughter who was lost and found again in *Pericles, Prince of Tyre*. This daughter, like the other young girls I have mentioned, restores the innocence and hope of a childhood scene, I suppose Cape Ann. She comes borne as it were by an *intermittence du coeur*:

What seas what shores what grey rocks and what islands
What water lapping the bow
And scent of pine and the woodthrush singing through
   the fog

What images return
O my daughter.

What she brings is "This grace dissolved in place." But in
the center of the remembered scene of childhood innocence,
intense as an electric filament, the very evil vibrates which
the scene forgives:

Those who sharpen the tooth of the dog, meaning
Death
Those who glitter with the glory of the hummingbird,
    meaning
Death
Those who sit in the stye of contentment, meaning
Death
Those who suffer the ecstasy of the animals, meaning
Death

The energy of the pasage, and its contrast with its setting,
are Dantesque. And it corresponds, in the design of the
poem, to irruptions of evil in Dante's Eden, for example
(Canto xxxii, line 130):

Poi parve a me che la terra s'aprisse
    tr'ambo le rote, e vidi uscirne un drago,
    che per lo carro su la coda fisse;
e, come vespa che ritragge l'ago,
    a sè traendo la coda maligna,
    trasse del fondo e gissen vago vago.

(Then it seemed to me that the earth was split
    between the wheels, and I saw a dragon issue,
    who from below with his tail the car transfixed;
and like a wasp drawing back its stinger,
    drawing back to itself its vicious tail,
    dragged out the floor and went off vague and listless.)

I do not of course mean to say that Eliot's lyric is to be
compared at any length with the firm and majestic structure

of the *Paradiso Terrestre*. But the chord of feelings, here sounded so lightly, is analogous. And because the poet does not pretend to know any more about this experience than he intimately knows—*Quis hic locus? Quae regio? Quae mundi plaga?*—or see any more in it than he sees, his verses may help us to guess what Dante meant by his poetry.

ᕤ CHAPTER 23. MATELDA:
THE LETTER FOR THE SPIRIT

BEATRICE is not the guide to the *Paradiso Terrestre*. She is the center of those visions and presences whereby the object of Dante's faith is made sensuously perceptible. But the faith which Dante finds at the end of the purgatorial journey is unspeaking; and though Beatrice speaks, she speaks in words and signs which Dante can take in only literally, not really understand.

Matelda is Dante's and our guide to the *Paradiso Terrestre*. As the sun comes up in Eden, she replaces Statius and Virgil, explaining the scene, and showing the travellers where to go and what to do. The ancient poets had guided the Pilgrim with their philosophical and poetic learning, their insight sharpened by their awareness of the records of previous travellers; Matelda knows Eden as one native to that element, but she reveals it only in her being and her belief.

The commentators do not agree upon Matelda's precise "meaning." Probably she stands for the Active Life as distinguished from the Contemplative, for the Pilgrim apparently foresaw her in his dream on the threshold of Eden, as Leah, whose delight it is to gather flowers, while Rachel her contemplative sister is motionless before her mirror. Perhaps she is also the visionary fulfillment of a certain Grancontessa of Tuscany, as Beatrice is the truth, or fulfillment of Beatrice Portinari. Here in Eden, Matelda does seem to be complementary to Beatrice, as Leah in the dream is to Rachel. Where the experts are in disagreement about the meaning of one of Dante's figures, it is usually safest to assume that they are all partially right; for Dante composes with concrete and many-sided elements which, like real people, may have various meanings.

Meanwhile we have Matelda herself, as Dante first presents her in the music and imagery of his verse. I tried to suggest in the last chapter how she is a creature of the classical Golden Age (Proserpine, perhaps, as the Pilgrim suggests), but reborn in the Christian saeculum; a fulfillment both of that ancient myth and of the lyric inspiration of Dante's own early poetry. She is the genius of the timeless earthly paradise (Canto xxviii, line 80):

"ma luce rende il salmo *Delectasti*"

("but the psalm *Delectasti* gives you light")

she says, meaning light on her being: "For thou, Lord, hast made me glad through thy work."

In the very first canto of the *Purgatorio* the Pilgrim, relieved of the nightmare of Hell, was made glad by the beauty of earth, the work of the Lord. The theme of his innocent pleasure in the world is one of the strands running through the whole *Antipurgatorio*. This theme, in its many subtle developments, foreshadows Matelda. It is in the unthinking pleasure the travellers take in Casella's song (Canto ii, line 115). It is in the literal and innocent obedience of the spirits in that realm (Canto iii, line 79):

Come le pecorelle escon del chiuso
   ad una, a due, a tre, e l'altre stanno
   timidette atterrando l'occhio e il muso

(Just as sheep come out of their enclosure
   singly, in twos, in threes, while the rest huddle
   timid, eyes and nose to the ground before them)

And it is in Virgil's prescription for the natural obedience which must precede illumination: "Be satisfied, you human race, with *quia*" (Canto iii, line 37); that is, accept the *what* of the world without demanding to know the *why*. So Matelda is obedient to the nature of this realm, before understanding; and so she guides the travellers and the reader through it. But, of course, the realm of the *Anti-*

purgatorio is like that of earth, while the *Paradiso Terrestre*
is the earth redeemed, or Eden as we have painfully *returned*
to it. The *Antipurgatorio* was only the figure; the *Paradiso
Terrestre* is the fulfillment.

For this reason the innocence, the obedience, and the delight of Matelda go deeper than anything in the *Antipurgatorio*. I have suggested that in the *Antipurgatorio* the Pilgrim had what Professor Maritain calls "poetic innocence,"
that obedience to a deep and direct mode of awareness which
is the inspiration of poetry, and the reliance of the most
sophisticated modern poets. Matelda is the spirit of this
poetic innocence; but what she is unthinkingly aware of is
not so much the world as the truth of the world—what the
world ought to be, and would be, if it were not obscured
and divided by the greedy passions of the human. In her,
"poetic innocence" and the innocence of faith, or belief, are
one. No wonder she must be a creature so idealized, she is
to guide us in an extremely rare, fine, and fleeting mode of
awareness, between the sad human knowledge of good and
evil one way, and the unseen beatific vision the other way,
where light will return to the mind (in the *Paradiso*) in a
new way altogether.

After our first impression of Matelda she is with us, sometimes seen, sometimes unseen, until the end of the canticle.
Dante has devised for her a role whereby her delicate being
is defined, and the anomalous experience of Eden is made to
hang together as though upon an almost imperceptible line
of melody. This he achieves, partly by the structure of the
actual scene, partly by the plot, or putting together of inci-
dents.

We know that when Dante enters Eden it is with a freedom of the whole being—all his feelings and perceptions—
such that he has now only to take his pleasure for his guide;
and his guide is Matelda. But Matelda is across the Stream,
and his pleasure in her voice and movement proceeds, not

toward the satisfaction of his sexual love, but toward the exploration of the scene of which she is the living epitome: "This 'harmony in the sentience' or harmony *of* the sentient, where the thought has its demarcation, the substance its *virtu*," as Mr. Pound says, defining the medieval feeling for the world redeemed. "What makes his art so wholly Christian," says Mr. Malraux of the classical Giotto, "is that the spiritual life proclaims its immanence on all these faces." We are held at that moment of the perception of beauty which precedes all the greedy deductions of the flesh; but this moment is neither static nor inhibited; charmed rather, like a dream, and alive with a harmony which the delights of the senses make and mean. No one actually dwells in Eden any more, says Saint Thomas Aquinas, but it is "not in vain, it shows the goodness of God, and all that man lost through sin."

Matelda (where we see and hear her beyond Lethe) explains the literal facts of her region, a real place, according to the tradition Dante followed, a garden lifted high above all earthly weather. But her words, at the same time, make us feel that "not with feet does one enter this garden, but with the feelings," as St. Bernard of Clairvaux said of the earthly paradise. Her mode of the spirit's life is immanent in all that she bids us see.

When the approach of the pageant of Revelation lights up the woods we have no eyes for Matelda, but it is she who gives us our clue (Canto xxix, line 15):

"Frate mio, guarda, ed ascolta"

("My brother, look, and listen")

she simply says; and again (line 62):

"Perchè pur ardi
sì nell'aspetto delle vive luci,
e ciò che vien di retro a lor non guardi?"

("Why do you burn
only in the sight of the vivid lights,
and to see what follows them you do not turn?")

She bids us be all in the vision, as it keeps unfolding, for all
meaning and spirit is *within* this evidence of the senses.

We are unaware of Matelda during the terrible scene with
Beatrice, unless the inhuman innocence of the angelic presences echoes Matelda's human innocence. But the scene is in
her style: the meaning (both anguish and beauty) is *in* the
Letter which Beatrice enforces. And because Dante is obedient to that, at a level of his being deeper than thought or will,
the course of his human passion is held as it was by Matelda's
beauty-across-the-stream. He feels "the great power of ancient
love" (line 39); he "knows the signs of the ancient flame"
(line 48). But he does not interpret it to suit his faithless
human greed; he feels *it*—not as the trigger reflexes of spe-
cifically sexual desire, but as a *virtu* touching the quick of
his *whole* being.

Dante loses consciousness at the end of the Beatrice scene,
but returns to himself (Canto XXXI, line 91), held by Matelda's innocent beauty in Lethe; and then he is made by her
to drink its waters. It was that spirit which led him (all the
way from the New Life of childhood) to Beatrice; and now
he has only that to cling to, as the memories of treachery
dissolve like melting ice, or wash away in the stream.

Matelda's touch after Lethe restores Dante for the two
related visions, of Beatrice with the Griffon doubly flashing
in her eyes, and of the ideal beauty of the human commu-
nity; after which he is overcome again. He comes to himself
with Matelda bending over him (Canto XXXII, line 83), "who
before was guide to my steps along the stream." She shows
him Beatrice mourning beneath the withered tree, and is
herself lost to sight again.

The effect of Matelda's returns—with a word, a gesture
or a touch—is to keep Dante and the reader on that fine line

which leads from one vision of Eden to the next contrasting one. Her guidance or coaching keeps directing us to a *moto spiritale* which may be described as immediate obedience: a complete psychic movement of acceptance, before the reason has made its definitions, before the will can envisage choices, even before the desires are differentiated. She is possible only in Eden, for only here can poetic innocence and the innocence of faith be one; only here is the Letter of the scene immediately true. She is thus the clue not only for the Pilgrim within the fiction, but for the reader, whose attention she directs to the peculiar style in which the *Paradiso Terrestre* is written: a style at once literal and visionary. But the best place in which to study these matters is Canto xxxiii, where all the threads are brought together.

Canto xxxiii opens after the Giant has dragged the Harlot off into the woods, leaving them empty. Beatrice is seen surrounded by the seven virtues, and grieving. The mystery of the vision of Eden is epitomized in the contrast between the music of the seven ladies and Beatrice's grief and anger; and then in her quotation from John 16.16: "A little while, and ye shall not see me; and again, a little while, and ye shall see me." In the second movement Beatrice slowly resumes her progress through the Garden, followed by the virtues and Dante and Statius who obey her slightest gesture. As she goes she prophesies that the corruption figured in the nightmare images of the last canto will be ended by a new ruler; but Dante, though he hears, does not understand her words. In the last movement the procession comes to a stop at Eunoe, the stream which restores all memory of good; and Matelda leads Dante to drink of its waters.

In this canto the underlying motive which sustained us through the journey of purgation slows down, and comes to its final stop. This movement was swiftest toward the end of the third Day, paused before the flame guarding Eden, and again, more completely, during the scene with Beatrice. Here we feel the slowing, not only in the narrative and in the

rhythmic scheme of the canto as a whole, but in the imagery:
the mind which turns to stone, the sun which seems motionless at noon, the streams which regretfully part. It is the
lingering feel of an aftermath, and a final reckoning.

Beatrice in effect says so when she invites Dante, who
follows her as though sleep-walking, to receive the answers
(line 23). Her speech contains the moral of the tale, but it
is in a sign-language which Dante cannot follow. The identity
of the new ruler whom she prophesies, the "five hundred,
ten and five," DXV, is still a favorite puzzle for the ingenious
and the erudite. The immediate effect of her whole speech,
with its apparently unconnected images—the sop God does
not fear, the mysterious numbers or letters, the petrifying
waters of the Elsa, Pyramus and his mulberry, the palmer
and his palm-frond—is like that of a landscape by Dali: an
odd assortment of properties bathed in a knowing light
which is not quite the natural light of earth. This effect is, of
course, intended, as Beatrice rather cruelly explains (line 85):

"Perchè conoschi," disse, "quella scuola
    ch'hai seguitata, e veggi sua dottrina
    come può seguitar la mia parola."

("So that you may understand that school," she said,
    "which you have followed, and see how far its teaching
    is capable of following my word.")

The school is that of Virgil, whose understanding has led
Dante (and the reader) to Eden; but this understanding does
not avail to *interpret* that vision. To Virgil's pagan eyes the
vision of earthly felicity is an impermeable barrier, the ceiling
which encloses the vast theatre of purgation. Virgil's wisdom would be to harden the mind and to quiet without hope
his desire—that insatiable natural thirst which drove us here.
But to the eye of Love—to Beatrice—the beauty of Eden is
transparent, and she can pass through it as through a window

to Heaven itself. Dante cannot follow her there as he is; he must be made over by Eunoe, and that is another story.

No further understanding is possible here; but we may consider the Pilgrim as he is at the end of his purgation, and Matelda, the clue to his curious mode of being.

Dante, a mortal man who in the flesh saw Eden, after Hell, after the labors of moral enlightenment, is now "bound by fear and shame" and "speaks as one dreaming" (lines 31-33). His "wit sleeps"—even the wit formed by Virgil, which does give moral meaning (line 64 ff.). His mind is "turned to stone" (line 74); it is "wax under the seal" (line 79). I suppose earthly felicity, innocence, must look so to us, with our very un-innocent sense of life: it must look less or more than human, as we understand the word. Dante enforces that impression, with his metaphors of wax and stone and somnambulism.

But Matelda is the life in this so fine, so undefinable moment of awareness; and if it *could* be defined, the phrase which introduces her final guidance would do so (line 130):

Com'anima gentil che non fa scusa,
    ma fa sua voglia della voglia altrui,
    tosto ch'ell'è per segno fuor dischiusa

(As a gentle soul who does not propose
    excuse, but makes her will of another's will
    as soon as it is in outward sign disclosed)

The delicate life is here caught from without, as something *Édénique* may sometimes be reflected for us in the unthinking response of a child. Matelda obeys a sign of Beatrice's; and Beatrice herself is a sign of Christ, the "will of another" which is hidden but effective here, as it has been at various points in the whole journey.

But the essence of Matelda is that, with her innocence of belief and of the poetic intuition together, she *can* take the sign, or letter, for the spirit. That is what Dante must do (as

Beatrice tells him) when he comes to tell of Eden in his poem
(line 76):

> "voglio anche, e se non scritto, almen dipinto,
>   che il te ne porti dentro a te, per quello
>   che si reca il bordon di palma cinto."

> ("and I wish you to take it back, pictured at least
>   within you, if not written, for the reason
>   that the pilgrim brings back his staff palm-wreathed.")

The reader also, if he is to feel the curious effect—a sort of
"double-take"—whereby the journey and the poem end together, must dwell upon the Letter of this final canto.

When I say that Matelda takes the Letter for the Spirit, I
am thinking of the *various* ways in which Dante employs the
Letter, or the literal, in the dramaturgy of his *Paradiso
Terrestre*. Beatrice's words, for example, which the Pilgrim
gets but does not understand, are a kind of Letter. But so,
on the other hand, is all that we see and hear and feel in
Eden: the scene, the procession, Matelda, Beatrice—all the
dramatis personae and what they do and say. Men write
only with language and the arts of language, while God
writes with nature and human history, according to Dante's
tradition; His Letters are themselves real and immediately
true. But Dante's poem is devised as a reflection and imitation of God's writing; and its scenes, therefore, are Letters
requiring interpretation. This applies particularly to Eden,
where God's writing is not obscured by human error. But it
also applies to the whole *Commedia*. Whenever the Pilgrim's spirit changes, he sees a new scene, and new Letter,
first as Letter only; and then by an act of his own spirit, he
grasps by imitation, or sympathetic identification, the Spirit
which made that particular visible (literal) sign. That is the
act of interpretation, and the moment of change; it coincides
with the appearance of a new and literally perceptible scene,
calling for a new act of the Pilgrim's spirit whereby God

will be obeyed (or imitated) in a new way. The end of this process would be when the Pilgrim's spirit coincided with God's; but Dante knew that that could not happen. He knew that his vision was not God's, and that he was writing a poem, not creating the universe. That is why, even at the end of the *Paradiso*, Dante, like Matelda, can only offer *that* miraculous Letter for the Spirit which is so far beyond it. And that is why the whole poem, in its literal clarity, is always at an end—a limit of human vision and spiritual capacity—yet at the same time pointing ahead.

But what ends here in Canto xxxiii is that underlying *moto spiritale*, growing and developing from one scene to another, which we have been trying to trace from the beginning of the canticle. "Per correr miglior acqua," Dante said in the first line: "to course over better waters." It is the human aspiration for the Good which we have been following upward: that love which moves all who are not permanently lost. Under Virgil's guidance that love learned to see itself in its own natural light: Eros, the insatiable natural thirst. During the third Day many upward-pointing signs suggested that this love was neither its own source nor its own end; that Agape was behind Eros. But though the Pilgrim could obey the signs, he could not understand the Force behind them in the light of nature; he proceeded still, applying to Virgil and Statius for help, as though Eros alone moved him. So he reaches Eden: a vision which ends the movement of Eros both as its fulfillment and as its denial. The aspiration which brought us here is either satisfied, or spent, or both. The vision does not dissolve, but is held at the Letter. For interpretation, seeing *through* the literal vision, would require an act of the Pilgrim's spirit obedient to the Spirit that made Eden; and that Spirit is not man's, but God's; not the human love which led us hither, but an unseen Force which will have to give the Pilgrim's spirit a new direction and a new movement before he can take in its light—*La Gloria di Colui che tutto move*, "The glory of

Him who moves all," as the first line of the *Paradiso* will put it. Here we can only be, like Matelda, more and less than human—obedient, not to the Spirit, but to the impermeable mystery of the beautiful Letter which it wrote here at the summit of the Mountain.

The sense of this mystery is heavy in the simple narrative which ends the canto (line 103):

E più corrusco, e con più lenti passi,
   teneva il sole il cerchio di merigge,
   che qua e là, come gli aspetti, fassi,
quando s'affisser, sì come s'affigge
   chi va dinanzi a gente per iscorta,
   se trova novitate o sue vestigge,
le sette donne al fin d'un'ombra smorta,
   qual sotto foglie verdi e rami nigri
   sopra suoi freddi rivi l'Alpe porta.

(And both more glowing, and with steps more slow,
   the sun was holding the arc of his noon ascent,
   which moves, as the aspect makes it, to and fro,
when came to rest, as one is wont to rest
   who goes ahead of people to escort them
   and finds there something strange or trace it left,
those seven ladies at a pale shadow's margin,
   such as beneath green leaves and dark branches
   the Alp extends over his cool torrents.)

They have reached the spring whence Lethe and Eunoe part "like friends that linger," and Matelda, obedient to the sign of the will of Another, makes Dante drink the water that will restore all memory of good. He would have liked to sing of that draught (line 139 ff.):

ma perchè piene son tutte le carte
   ordite a questa Cantica seconda,
   non mi lascia più ir lo fren dell'arte.

(but because the pages all are filled up now
 which were ordained for this second canticle,
 the curb of art lets me go on no more.)

The Pilgrim who made the journey, the man who recorded
it in the second canticle, and the reader who has uncertainly
followed, are left together here, while a new movement of
spirit into an unseen realm is lightly mentioned:

Io ritornai dalla santissim'onda
 rifatto sì, come piante novelle
 rinnovellate di novella fronda,
puro e disposto a salire alle stelle.

(I came back out of the most holy stream
 remade, in the same way that new trees are
 when they have been renewed in their new leaf,
clean and made ready to rise to the stars.)

✌ NOTES

My PURPOSE in offering these notes is to enable the reader to pursue some of the questions touched on in the text a little farther. They are divided into two sections: works used throughout these studies and notes on the text.

I. WORKS USED
THROUGHOUT THESE STUDIES

1. *The Works of Dante Alighieri.* The Temple Classics. London: J. M. Dent and Sons, Ltd., 1900—.

All of Dante's works are available in translation in this edition, which is indispensable for English-speaking readers of Dante. The three volumes devoted to the *Divine Comedy* are printed with the Italian text and a prose translation on facing pages. The translation takes very few liberties with the literal meaning of the original; and because the Italian is always there, the reader soon finds himself reading it. The arguments prefixed to each canto are very useful in early readings. The notes in all of the works are excellent. They provide all the information which most readers require; they contain many valuable references to Dante's sources and to relevant passages in his own works; and they indicate (usually without trying to solve) the chief problems of interpretation.

2. "Dante," by T. S. Eliot. In *Selected Essays, 1917-1932.* New York: Harcourt Brace and Co., 1932.

"Talk on Dante," by T. S. Eliot. *Kenyon Review*, Vol. XIV, No. 2, Spring 1952.

Mr. Eliot's essay on Dante is the best introduction to his poetry. His "Talk on Dante" traces the master's influences on his own poetry—which is itself a bridge to Dante.

3. *Distinguer pour Unir, ou Les Degrés du Savoir*, by Jacques Maritain. Paris: Desclés de Brouwer et Cie., 1932.

Situation de la Poésie, by Jacques and Raissa Maritain. Paris: Desclés de Brouwer et Cie., 1938.

"Le Songe de Descartes," by Jacques Maritain. Paris: Corréa, 1932.

Creative Intuition in Art and Poetry, by Jacques Maritain. New York: Bollingen Series, Pantheon Books, 1953.

The title of Professor Maritain's major philosophical work suggests the kinship between his principles of thought and Dante's principles of composition. Because Professor Maritain actually uses and develops Thomistic philosophy in our time, he gives us access to Dante's world and to his philosophical and theological culture. My reading of Dante has been accompanied and guided by Maritain for many years, and I owe him a debt which continues to accumulate.

The Maritains' studies of poetry are based on that fundamental strand in contemporary culture, French poetry since Baudelaire. They illuminate poetry "in itself"; and by showing what modern poetry is, free us to consider Dante's unique conception of the art.

4. *Dante als Dichter der Irdischen Welt*, by Erich Auerbach. Berlin und Leipzig: Verlag Walter de Gruyter & Co., 1929.

Neue Dantestudien: Sacrae Scripturae Sermo Humilis; Figura; Franz von Assisi in der Komödie, by Erich Auerbach. Istanbul: Istanbuler Schriften, 1944.

Mimesis, by Erich Auerbach. Bern: A. Francke AG. Verlag, 1946. (This work has been translated into English by Willard R. Trask: *Mimesis: The Representation of Reality in Western Literature*, by Erich Auerbach. Princeton, New Jersey: Princeton University Press, 1953.)

5. *An Essay on the Vita Nuova*, by Charles Singleton. Cambridge, Mass.: Harvard University Press, 1949.

"Dante and Myth," by Charles Singleton. *Journal of the History of Ideas*, Vol. x, No. 4, October 1949.

"Dante's Allegory," by Charles Singleton, *Speculum*, Vol. xxv, No. 1, January 1950.

"Dante's *Comedy*: The Pattern at the Center," by Charles Singleton. *Romanic Review*, Vol. xlii, No. 3, October 1951.

The works listed above, by authorities on Dante, are useful for my purposes because they directly illuminate the text itself. I have used them, not only for particular passages, but as guides to the whole form and style of the *Commedia*.

II. NOTES ON THE TEXT

PART ONE

Chapter 1.

"Can Grande." The quotation is from the *Letter* he wrote dedicating the *Paradiso* to his patron. It will be found, in translation, in *Latin Works of Dante Alighieri* (The Temple Classics, London: J. M. Dent and Sons, Ltd., 1929), page 351. The *Letter* is a concentrated work, and not easy reading, but it contains many useful explanations of the purpose and style of the *Commedia*. I have used it again and again in these studies.

"Metaphor of the Journey." There is a very clear analysis of Dante's complex use of this metaphor in the beginning of the *Inferno* in "The Other Journey," by Charles Singleton (*Kenyon Review*, Vol. xiv, No. 2, Spring 1952).

"Myths of prehistoric culture-heroes." We are only beginning to see how much mythic lore underlies the *Comedy* in one way or another. There are references to it in *The Timeless Theme*, by Colin Still (London: Ivor Nicholson & Watson, 1936), page 97 and passim. *Die Jenseitsvorstellungen vor Dante*, by Dr. August Rüegg (Cologne: Verlagsanstalt Benziger & Co., 1945), is a collection of legends of journeys to the other world which bear some resemblance to Dante's, many of which Dante may have known. I do not think Dr. Rüegg's book is at all complete—it does not, for instance, describe Arabic parallels—but it shows the kind of research that is possible in this field.

"The *Paradiso*." The reader can see the importance of the *Paradiso* for a complete understanding of the *Comedy* in Auerbach's *Dante als Dichter* or in *Poetica e Poesia di Dante*, by Francesco Biondolillo (Messina: Casa Editrice G. d'Anna, 1948), a very useful introduction to the reading of the *Comedy*. *Symbolism in Medieval Thought*, by H. F. Dunbar (New Haven: Yale University Press, 1929) is a much more ambitious study of the whole symbolism of the *Comedy* as culminating in the third canticle. See also "The Symbolic Imagination," by Allen Tate, *Kenyon Review*, Vol. xiv, No. 2, Spring 1952.

"Professor Maritain." cf. "Dante's Innocence and Luck," by Jacques Maritain, *Kenyon Review*, Vol. xiv, No. 2, Spring 1952.

"Professor Curtius." The reference is to *Europäische Literatur and Lateinisches Mittelalter*, by Ernst Robert Curtius (Bern: A. Francke AG. Verlag, 1948). Professor Curtius has comparatively little to say directly about Dante, but his monumental study shows the centrality of Dante's culture. I mention it here in case the reader may wish documentation—but the erudite problems are beyond my capacity and the purpose of my studies. See below for further references to this work.

"Shelley." Shelley says: "The poetry of Dante may be considered as the bridge thrown over the stream of time, which unites the modern and ancient world." From "The Defense of Poetry," page 511 in *The Selected Poetry and Prose of Percy Bysshe Shelley*, ed. by Carlos Baker (New York: The Modern Library, 1951).

"Eliot." *Selected Essays*, page 225.

"with the revolutionary movements of the early romantics." Our modern reading of Dante, like so much else in our literary culture, started to develop in that period. "Dante in der deutschen Romantik," by Clara-Charlotte Fuchs, in *Deutsches Dantejahrbuch*, 15 Band, is a useful collection. I owe this reference to Professor Auerbach.

"Henry James." James's theory of the central intelligence is scattered throughout his Prefaces. He says, for example, about *Roderick Hudson*: "The center of interest throughout 'Roderick' is in Rowland Mallet's consciousness, and the drama is the very drama of that consciousness." Page 16, *The Art of the Novel, Critical Prefaces*, by Henry James, with an Introduction by R. P. Blackmur. (New York: Charles Scribner's Sons, 1947.)

Chapter 3.

"T. S. Eliot in his book on Dante." *op.cit.*, page 199.

"Chekhov's second acts." I have pointed out parallels between Chekhov's drama and this part of the *Purgatorio* in *The Idea of a*

Theater (Princeton, New Jersey: Princeton University Press, 1949), pages 166 and 172.

"Croce, in his reading of the *Commedia.*" *La Poesia di Dante,* by Benedetto Croce (Bari: Gius. Laterza & Figli, 1921).

Chapter 4.

"Coleridge's famous distinction." I have taken these quotations from page 86, *Coleridge on Imagination,* by I. A. Richards (New York: Harcourt Brace & Co., 1935). Mr. Richards' book is a very useful study of Coleridge's poetic theory. I have used it especially in connection with the first two Days of the *Purgatorio* where the kinship between the Pilgrim's sensibility and that of modern poetry is closest.

Chapter 5.

"Eliot remarks." *op.cit.,* page 207. Speaking of Paolo and Francesca, he says: "Taking such an episode by itself, we can get as much out of it as we get from the reading of a whole single play of Shakespeare." I do not mean to make Mr. Eliot responsible for my views on the coherence of the canto.

PART TWO

Chapter 6.

"Coleridge." This quotation also is taken from Mr. Richard's book (*op.cit.,* page 139; it is from *The Statesman's Manual,* Appendix B). It is very interesting to compare Coleridge's philosophy of poetry as expounded by Richards—a "principle of sane growth in the mind," as Mr. Richards says—with Dante's poetics as it slowly emerges in the course of the *Purgatorio.* There is a romantic basis in Dante's practice as a poet, but unlike modern poets he worked out for himself a vital relationship to history and tradition and, of course, to religious faith. He has a very modern reliance upon his own feelings and perceptions, but by the time he wrote the *Commedia* he had combined that with a very un-modern respect for the achievements of the past.

"Professor Curtius's great study." *op.cit.* The quotations (which I have translated) are from page 26.

Chapter 7.

"*poiema, pathema, mathema.*" This phrase is taken from *A Grammar of Motives*, by Kenneth Burke (New York: Prentice-Hall, Inc., 1945). See pages 264-265.

"Plato and Aristotle." I am thinking of Aristotle's *Nicomachean Ethics* and Plato's *Republic*. The Loeb Classical Library (New York: G. P. Putnam's Sons) is convenient for those with a little Greek. Mr. Wheelright's *Aristotle*, a good selection in very clear translation, is good for those with no Greek (*Aristotle*, ed. by Philip Wheelwright. New York: Odyssey Press, 1951. Enlarged edition).

"The progressive educators." The most enlightened short statement I know of the theory of progressive education is *The Art and Practice of Teaching*, by William H. Kilpatrick (New York: William R. Scott, 1937). The progressive educators rediscovered many ancient principles of the psychology of learning but have never succeeded in making a curriculum. There is a significant parallel between their insights and those of modern poets: they are true to individual experience but historically nowhere, and anarchic in relation to the cultural heritage.

"The form of Sophoclean tragedy." cf. *The Idea of a Theater*, page 39, "Analogues of the Tragic Rhythm."

"pity, which joins him to the human sufferer." This is Stephen Dedalus's explanation of Aristotle's definition of tragedy, page 239, in *A Portrait of the Artist as a Young Man*, by James Joyce, with an introduction by Herbert Gorman (New York: The Modern Library, 1928).

"action-scene ratio." See *A Grammar of Motives*, page 3 and passim.

"Aristotle's rule of thumb." Book II of the *Nicomachean Ethics* expounds virtuous conduct as a mean between opposite excesses. Aristotle's use of the passage between Scylla and Charybdis is on page 110, Loeb Classics edition.

Chapter 8.

"Boethius." See for example *Convivio*, Temple Classics edition, pages 144-146, where Dante discusses the mind and the light of philosophy with reference to Aristotle and to Boethius' *De Consolatione Philosophiae*. The *Convivio* is the monument of Dante's own effort to live by philosophy, which this part of the *Purgatorio* reflects. cf. Chapters 11 and 12 below.

Chapter 9.

"The first is bound, the latter uncommitted." In the reading of Dante's line (*Purgatorio*, Canto IV, line 12):

> questa è quasi legata, e quella è sciolta

I have followed the Temple Classics edition, in which *questa* is translated "former" and *quella* "latter." Scartazzini gives the opposite interpretation of *questa* and *quella*. I am not qualified to discuss the syntactical question, but it seems to me, on the basis of the whole context, that Dante is saying that a strong sensory impression (sight or sound) binds that faculty but not the soul as a whole. We have seen that occur when the Pilgrim was caught by the sweetness of Casella's song (Canto II, lines 115 ff.). On either reading we get a picture of the psyche absorbed in one of its faculties while the rest are unused. The distinction is between the momentary actuality of the soul's life and its wider potentialities, which can only be fully realized if it gets the beatific vision. cf. Temple Classics edition, page 46, note, and Giovanni Andrea Scartazzini, *La Divina Commedia, Testo Critico Riveduto, Col Commento Scartazziniano, Rifato da Giuseppe Vandelli* (Milan: Ulrico Hoepli, editore, 1938), page 326, note.

"Aristotle." Aristotle's remarks on reason and anger can be found in the *Nicomachean Ethics*, VII, VI ff.

"Mr. Philip Wheelwright." *op.cit.*, passim.

"*De Monarchia.*" Both this work and the *Convivio* help one to understand the moral and political philosophy of these cantos. But they, of course, are discursive works, while the *Purgatorio*, much more concentrated and allusive, has the concreteness and the elaborately-composed contexts of drama.

"The struggle . . . expounded by thinkers of various persuasions." I am thinking, for example, of Ortega y Gasset. Maritain has made many illuminating analyses of modern rationalism (*op.cit.* and *Le Songe de Descartes*). From an entirely different point of view, John Dewey or D. H. Lawrence complain of our loss of a rounded conception of the human, and often blame our intellectualism for it. But the list could be indefinitely extended.

"Pascal." See, for example, "The Triumph of Evil in Pascal," by Erich Auerbach, *Hudson Review*, Vol. IV, No. I, Spring 1951. Professor Auerbach analyzes one of Pascal's *Pensées*, that on *La Force et la Justice*; and the reader, I think, must be struck by the similarity between Pascal's thought and its atmosphere of surrounding darkness and the Pilgrim's first exchanges with Marco Lombardo.

Chapter 11.

"Aristotle's notion of *praxis*." The quotation is taken from Aristotle's *Theory of Poetry and Fine Art, with a Critical Text and Translation of the Poetics*, by S. H. Butcher, M.P. (London: Macmillan & Co., Ltd., 1932, fourth edition), page 27, VI, 9. Butcher's edition, with his commentary and with his translation of the Greek on facing pages, is most useful.

I have used the analogical concept of action in *The Idea of a Theater* in the analysis of various kinds of drama. See, for example, page 35, "The Imitation of an Action"; page 48, "The Rational Imitation of Action"; page 229, "Plot and Action"; and page 236, "Mimetic Perception of Action."

"Dante's generation confirmed, but amplified . . . the ancient soul's knowledge of itself." I am thinking of St. Thomas Aquinas's developments of Aristotle's notions. See, for example, *On Being and Essence*, by St. Thomas Aquinas, translated with an Introduction and Notes by Armand Maurer, C.S.B., M.A., Ph.D., L.M.S. (Toronto: Pontifical Institute of Medieval Studies, 1949), Chapter IV, page 43, "Essence as Found in Separate Substances." In the translator's Introduction, Aquinas's "revolution in metaphysics" is described as follows (page 9): "That revolution can be summed up briefly as a turning of the metaphysician's interest from form and essence, where it had lingered for so many centuries, to the act of existing. For the Greeks, an explanation in terms of essence or nature was always considered the last word of the philosopher. . . . It was a decisive moment in the history of metaphysics when philosophers became aware of the specific problems which attach to existence as distinct from essence." Something very much like this "revolution" is dramatized during the third Day on the Mountain, when the Pilgrim, in the light of Virgil's timeless and general knowledge of the soul's life, is made sharply aware of the "existentialist" problems of his own life in its historic time and place.

"Dante's symbolism." Eliot distinguishes between Shakespeare's metaphors and Dante's as follows (*op.cit.*, page 205): "But whereas the simile of Dante is merely to make you see more clearly how the people looked, and is explanatory, the figure of Shakespeare is expansive rather than intensive; its purpose is to *add* to what you see. . . . It is more elusive, and it is less possible to convey without close knowledge of the English language. . . . But as the whole poem of Dante is, if you like, one vast metaphor, there is hardly any place for metaphor in the detail of it." Mr. Eliot's diagnosis is accurate. The moon in this canto is not a metaphor unless the whole journey is. But because the moon reappears in so many contexts in the carefully composed scenes of the fictive journey, it has overtones of meaning—an "expansive" effect—like that of Shakespeare's metaphors.

Chapter 12.

"Philosophy." *Convivio*, Temple Classics edition, page 237.

"Philip Wicksteed." *Convivio*, page 430.

"The struggle . . . behind . . . the *Convivio*." cf. Biondolillo, *Poetica e Poesia di Dante* (*op.cit.*), page 88 ff., "Le canzoni dell'Amore razionale."

"Babbitt's Humanism." Eliot's discussion of this movement (in *Selected Essays*) in his two essays on Babbitt, is a critique of humanism in general, closely related to some of the issues in this part of the *Purgatorio*.

"allegory of theologians." The nature of Dante's use of this allegory is still being explored. The reader who wishes to go into this matter should read Singleton's "Dante's Allegory," a discussion of Dante's change from the allegory of poets of the *Convivio* to the different allegory of the *Commedia*. Auerbach's *Figura* is an indispensable study of the development of Dante's allegory. I shall refer to this problem again in the third and fourth parts of this book.

"Christian drama . . . of man's life in history." The question of Dante's view of history is also far from settled. One of the best places to study it is in *Purgatorio*, Cantos xx-xxxiii. I shall have much to say of it below. In the meantime, a reader who wishes a very good general discussion of Christian views of history should consult *Faith and History*, by Reinhold Niebuhr (New York: Charles Scribner's Sons, 1949). Professor Niebuhr has his own point of view, and he does not mention Dante here; but his book is a very enlightened account of the chief issues, many of which underlie the drama of the third Day in Purgatory. St. Augustine's *The City of God* is, of course, the foundation of Christian historiography.

PART THREE

Chapter 15.

"Professor Curtius." *op.cit.*, page 26. My translation.

"The allegory of poets." This is the phrase in the *Convivio* to which I referred in Part Two. The reader is also reminded of Singleton's "Dante's Allegory."

"*Figura*," by Auerbach. This is Professor Auerbach's most extended historic analysis of the method. He also expounds it in *Mimesis*, and the reader can find a number of citations in the index of that work. The quotations from *Figura* were translated by me.

"Tradition and the Individual Talent," by Eliot. *op.cit.*, page 6.

"Dante regarded his poem as fictive." I realize that this is a very controversial point. I am not too happy with this way of putting it; the word "fictive" in our usage almost implies disbelief, which is not what I am trying to say. I do not think that Dante believed he had actually descended to the center of the earth and risen beyond the sun. It is equally clear that he believed that the *Comedy* meant something true, far beyond the illustrative, philosophical truth of his "poetic allegory." The reader will find a good discussion of the matter in Singleton's "Dante's Allegory."

"Dante's conception of history." Another large and controversial topic. Whatever Dante's history may be, it is clear that the growth of his Christian philosophy of history is dramatized during the third Day and the morning of the fourth Day of the *Purgatorio*. See Professor Niebuhr's book (*op.cit.*), especially his distinction between Christian and classic conceptions of history.

Chapter 16.

"The fragrant trees." The notes in the Temple Classics edition indicate some of the chief problems of interpretation on these trees. There is also a discussion of them in *Die Jenseitsvorstellungen vor Dante*, by August Rüegg (*op.cit.*), II Band, page 100.

"Use Dante makes of the symbol." The reader who may wish to pursue the complexities of Dante's symbolism should consult Dunbar's *Medieval Symbolism* (*op.cit.*). "Types of Association," page 475, and "Basis of Symbolism in Functional Truth of Letter," page 490, are particularly relevant to this part of the *Purgatorio*.

"Father Daniélou." "The Problem of Symbolism," in *Thought*, Vol. xxv, No. 98, September 1950.

Chapter 17.

"Not of Eros, but of Agape." See *Agape and Eros* by Anders Nygren (New York: Macmillan & Co., 1937-1939). The thesis of this book is the unbridgeable difference between God's love and man's. Dr. Nygren is less subtle and more extreme than Dante, but his book is a powerful statement of a classic paradox of Christian faith and so relevant here.

"philosophic issues . . . reflected . . . in the practice of poets."

The notes in the Temple Classics edition contain valuable references to the philosophical disputes reflected in this passage. A very illuminating discussion of poets of Dante's school, and of their various more or less heretical philosophies, can be found in *Dante Creatore del Dolce Stil Nuovo*, by Francesco Biondolillo (Palermo: Casa Editrice Trimarchi, 1937).

Chapter 18.

"Dolce stil nuovo." This chapter owes a great deal to Singleton's *Essay on the Vita Nuova*. Dante's early work, celebrating the love of Beatrice, may be regarded as a small, abstract sketch of the central theme, the epic of love, of the *Comedy*. Much that Professor Singleton has to say about the transformations of love in that work, its complex and sophisticated form, and the subtle relations between the author, his book, and its subject, apply by analogy to the *Comedy*.

I have also derived understanding and encouragement from the work of Professor Biondolillo, which I have already cited. The present chapter is an attempt to apply a principle which he explains as follows in *Poetica e Poesia di Dante*: "The true esthetics of Dante is, strictly speaking, not in his scattered observations of a theoretical nature . . . but it is in that work in which his whole soul expresses itself . . . I mean in the *Divine Comedy*, in a poem and not in a work of abstract philosophy." (page 2) "It is necessary to understand Dante's esthetics in action: that is, his poetics." (page 3) (My translations.)

"*confuses paroles.*" From Baudelaire's *Correspondances*.

"Professor Maritain." His latest work on poetry, *Creative Intuition in Art and Poetry*.

"Stephen Dedalus." His remark in *A Portrait of the Artist as a Young Man* (*op.cit.*), page 250. The stress which the best modern poets lay upon the uniqueness and independence of the pleasures and intuitions of poetry could be illustrated at great length.

"poetry of poetries." Compare Hugo von Hofmannsthal: "The higher man is the unification of many men, the higher work of poetry requires, for its production, many poets in one." Quoted by Curtius, *op.cit.*, page 151 (my translation). Curtius' whole passage on the theocentric drama of the Middle Ages throws much light on Dante's poetics.

"Professor Curtius." *op.cit.* Professor Curtius' work is a vast mine of information and insight for Dante's literary culture and its relation to faith and theology. The reader is referred especially to Chapter 12, page 219, "Poesie und Theologie," and Chapter 17, page 352, "Dante."

"Dante's style . . . seems to contain all the modes of discourse." See "Dante's Ten Terms for the Treatment of the Treatise," by R. P. Blackmur, *Kenyon Review*, Vol. xiv, No. 2, Spring 1952. Professor Blackmur explores the possible relationships and combinations of these modes in a single conception of language.

"Saint Bonaventura." See *Saint Bonaventura's De Reductio Artium ad Theologiam, A Commentary with an Introduction and Translation*, by Sister Emma Thérèse Healy (St. Bonaventura College, 1939).

PART FOUR

Chapter 20.

"earthly life of Dante . . . and everyman's." I have no authority for the notion that the four Days of the *Purgatorio* reflect (among other things) a sequence from childhood to age. It seems to me to be shown in the poem itself. Dante discusses the four ages of man in *Convivio* (*op.cit.*), pages 342-375. But the doctrines of that work must be applied only with great care to the *Purgatorio*.

"*Essay on the Vita Nuova*," Chapter III of this work, "From Love to Caritas," and Chapter IV, "*Vita Nuova*," show how Dante's early work, like the *Comedy*, may be read as a drama of love's transformations. Professor Singleton's exposition is an indispensable account of Dante's uniquely self-conscious methods of composition, and his excellent notes illustrate Dante's manifold sources in the culture of his time.

"The medieval method of assigning four meanings to the

Scripture." The fourfold method is difficult to apply with any confidence, partly because it is differently used by different authors, partly because its use is an art which, like all arts, takes practice. I may refer to Singleton's "Dante's Allegory" and to Dunbar's *Medieval Symbolism* (*op.cit.*), especially "Method of Medieval Symbolic Usage," page 18, and "The Development of the Fourfold Interpretation," page 497. The rhyme I quoted defining the four meanings puts the Allegory before the Trope, while in the *Purgatorio* the Allegory is approached by way of the Trope. This I suppose reflects Dante's own *itinerarium mentis* from moral philosophy to faith; and it is consistent with the point he makes to Can Grande, that the *Comedy* in the whole and in its parts is governed by morals or ethics.

Chapter 21.

"The erudite are still exploring." The reader who may wish to sample the scholarly literature on the *Paradiso Terrestre* might start with the notes in the Temple Classics edition, or in Scartazzini (*op.cit.*). A very suggestive collection of possible sources of Dante's *Paradiso Terrestre* will be found in *Il Paradiso Terrestre Dantesco*, by Edoardo Coli (Florence: Tipografia G. Carnesecchi e Figli, 1897). I have already mentioned Rüegg's *Die Jenseitsvorstellungen vor Dante*, which adduces more literary and less theological predecessors than Coli. A brief glimpse of this jungle will show the reader why I make every effort to avoid the kinds of problems which *Wissenschaft* might be able to solve.

"Professor Singleton." "Dante's *Comedy*: The Pattern at the Center." This essay is indispensable. With regard to the form of the *Comedy* as a whole, however, I think two other different centers must be recognized: the center of Virgil's light, in *Purgatorio* XVII and XVIII, and the *Paradiso's* final ineffable vision of God—a "center" outside the poem.

"Eliot points out." *op.cit.*, page 224.

Chapter 22.

"Ezra Pound." *The Spirit of Romance*, by Ezra Pound, M.A. (London: J. M. Dent & Sons, Ltd., n.d.)

"Guido Cavalcanti." See *Guido Cavalcanti Rime* (Genoa: Edizioni Marsano S. A., 1931). This is Pound's expanded bilingual edition of Cavalcanti, with explanatory essays. The essay entitled "Medievalism" (from which I have quoted a few phrases) is another very interesting attempt to define the qualities of poetry of this period which Pound loved. All of his lore needs to be corrected by a reading of Biondolillo's *Dante Creatore del Dolce Stil Nuovo* or Singleton's observations on Dante's school in his *Essay on the Vita Nuova*. But Pound felt, and used in some of his own verse, a kinship with this period; and so his work offers us a bridge to the *stil novisti*.

"André Malraux." The quotations are from Malraux's study of Giotto and of classical parallels in medieval art, in *The Psychology of Art*, by André Malraux, translated by Stuart Gilbert (New York: Bollingen Series XXIV, 1949). See Vol. ii, pages 78-110. The first quotations are from pages 106-107; the second beginning "so long as the great movement . . ." will be found on pages 88-89.

"Charles Williams." *The Figure of Beatrice*, by Charles Williams (London: Faber & Faber, Ltd., 1943).

"*The Timeless Theme*," by Colin Still (*op.cit.*).

"*Marina.*" This poem can be found in *Collected Poems, 1909-1935*, by T. S. Eliot (New York: Harcourt Brace & Co., 1936).

Chapter 23.

"Mr. Pound." From "Medievalism," in *Guido Cavalcanti Rime*.

"Mr. Malraux." *op.cit.*

"Saint Thomas Aquinas." This quotation is taken from Coli's *Paradiso Terrestre Dantesco* (*op.cit.*), page 85.

"Saint Bernard." This quotation is also from Coli, page 76. In spite of what Saint Bernard said, Coli's review of Scholastic doctrine on the *Paradiso Terrestre* indicates that it was regarded as a real place, and Dante seems to combine this tradition with his own poetry and dramaturgy.

"five hundred, ten and five." See *The DXV Problem and the Veltro*, by J. H. Sacret (Reading: Bradley & Son, Ltd., 1937).

This is a review of the whole problem of the identity of the leader whom Beatrice seems to be prophesying so enigmatically. Sacret's study offers a good example of the difficulties one encounters in the attempt to attach the Letter of the *Comedy* to literal facts, past, present, or future. It also shows a dimension of Dante's structure, his number-symbolism in all its ramifications, which I have entirely neglected in these essays. What interests me in Beatrice's prophecy, however, is its style, which is certainly intended to puzzle both the Pilgrim and the reader.

"The Letter for the Spirit." It would perhaps not be too much to say that Dante's whole art, which was designed to convey God's truth, is in this relationship. The reader who may wish to consider how fundamental it is should remember Saint Paul's dictum, "The letter killeth, but the spirit giveth life." Saint Augustine's "On the Spirit and the Letter" in Volume i of *Basic Writings of St. Augustine*, edited with introduction and notes by Whitney J. Oates (New York: Random House, 1948) is a classic (if not *the* classic) elucidation of the relationship. See also *De Monarchia* (Temple Classics edition), page 237.